The Life Cycle of the Human Soul

Incarnation – Conception – Birth

Death – Hereafter – Reincarnation

ALSO BY RALPH METZNER

Birth of a Psychedelic Culture (2010: with Ram Dass and Gary Bravo)

Mind Space and TimeStream (2010)

Alchemical Divination (2009)

The Roots of War and Domination (2008)

The Expansion of Consciousness (2008)

Sacred Vine of Spirits – Ayahuasca (ed - 2006)

Sacred Mushroom of Visions – Teonanácatl (ed - 2005)

Green Psychology (1999)

The Unfolding Self (1998)

The Well of Remembrance (1994)

Through the Gateway of the Heart (ed - 1985)

Know Your Type (1979)

Maps of Consciousness (1971)

The Ecstatic Adventure (ed - 1968)

The Psychedelic Experience (1964; with Timothy Leary and Richard Alpert)

The Life Cycle of the Human Soul

Incarnation – Conception – Birth

Death – Hereafter – Reincarnation

by
Ralph Metzner

Green Earth Foundation
&
Regent Press

Copyright © 2011 by Ralph Metzner

All rights reserved.

ISBN 13: 978-1-58790-213-0
ISBN 10: 1-58790-213-3
Library of Congress Control Number: 2010943108

Graphics & Layout by Cynthia Smith
Cover Photo by Ralph Metzner

Published by
REGENT PRESS
www.regentpress.net
for
GREEN EARTH FOUNDATION
www.greenearthfound.org

Printed in the U.S.A.
REGENT PRESS
2747 Regent Street
Berkeley, CA 94705
e-mail: regentpress@mindspring.com

Printed on recycled paper

Contents

Introduction 1

1 Birth – Traumatic Realities, Ecstatic Potentials 11

2 Prenatal Imprints and Ancestral Connections 33

3 Death and Hereafter 57

4 Life Between Lives 81

5 From Incarnation to Conception and Rebirth 103

References and Select Bibliography 123

Appendix: On the mediumship of William Shakespeare 131

Introduction

In this book I will be discussing the experience of life before birth, and the experience of life after death of the physical body. Doing so transcends the assumed boundaries of the Western worldview of scientific materialism. Mainstream medicine and psychology do not believe there is any prenatal experience to talk about – and the mainstream agnostic worldview assumes that we can say nothing about life after death. Nevertheless, in the last fifty years in the West, there have been a number of new pioneering approaches for accessing these realms of consciousness that are at some remove from the presumed ordinary time-space reality.

As a radical empiricist in the tradition of William James, I do not exclude any experiences or observations from consideration, just because we can't account for them within the existing paradigms of reality. I prefer the approach of suspending my commitment to a particular paradigm, in order to consider the observations presented, my own and those of others, with impartiality. Inevitably, our reports and interpretations of subjective experience are bound up with our pre-existing worldviews and models of reality. Even in our ordinary, functional waking state it is not always a simple matter to distinguish what I am seeing (observation) from what I think about what I am seeing (interpretation).

This approach is what the Dalai Lama has called "first-person empiricism," an empiricism that is inclusive of the subjective realm of personal experience. In such an approach, reports of first-person subjective experience are objectively studied in relation and comparison to the reported experience of one or more other observers. In *Mind Space and Time Stream* I wrote that "a subjective experience communicated and recognized by at least one other person starts to become an objective observation. Hence: *subjective + 1 = objective*" (p. 22). We base our interpretations (as well as on-going re-interpretations) of reality on our own subjective experience, comparing and correlating them with what others have said or written about their own experience. In accord with the paradigms of empirical science, the accumulation of identical or similar observations from the same or additional observers increases the reliability of our findings and descriptions.

To even consider experience reports from pre-natal or post-mortem life as potential sources of new knowledge and understanding, requires a suspension of the prejudices of the generally accepted worldview of our culture and community. In ancient times in Western culture, and to this day in most Asian societies, concepts of the soul and of reincarnation have had a much deeper level of understanding, and were reflected in numerous myths and spiritual writings. For this reason, I will be including consideration of some classic texts of spiritual literature and mythology, including ancient Egyptian, Greek and Tibetan Buddhist, for insights into the pre-birth and after-death realms.

There are five main sources from which modern consciousness researchers have gathered observations and experiences beyond the thresholds of birth and death: psychedelic states; meditation and yoga; shamanic journeys; deep altered state hypnotherapy; states induced by non-ordinary breathing practices. I will discuss each of these methodologies in turn.

The use of *psychedelics* to explore non-ordinary realms of consciousness is the way I personally first became acquainted with these areas: through my participation in the studies of psychedelic drugs at Harvard University in the early 1960s, with Tim Leary and Richard Alpert (later Ram Dass). We had followed a suggestion of Aldous Huxley and adapted the teachings of the *Tibetan Book of the Dead* as the basis for our guidebook on psychedelic states, *The Psychedelic Experience*, first published in 1964. In the years since its publication, I have received many letters and comments to the effect that while most actual psychedelic experiences did not follow the idealized sequence of three stages laid out in the *Bardo Thödol,* what people appreciated about our manual were the recommendations to think of psychedelic experiences as an opportunity for psycho-spiritual practice and learning.

It is clear that the drugs *per se* do not produce or cause those experiences, rather they function as amplifiers of perception. The experiences and observations are a function of the intention or set of the individual, and the setting or context, as well as the preparation beforehand and interpretation afterwards. Because such drugs and related plants and fungi amplify and vivify perception, they have functioned for many people, including myself, as a first mind-opening foray into the realms of pre-birth, after-death and other-world experience. I will be drawing here on my own experiences with these substances, as well as reports of individuals with whom I have worked in guided divinations, both group and individual – where this was possible within the given legal-social framework of the time and place.

Meditation and yoga, especially the Tantric and Taoist forms, are the most wide-spread methods of accessing the non-ordinary realms of consciousness beyond time-space. Concentrative and mindfulness types of meditation are the experiential foundation of spiritual practice in the Asian religious traditions – and to a lesser extent also in the Western religions, although there the forms of faith and devotion generally predominate over psycho-spiritual practices. My experience with yogic practices was shaped by the ten years of full-time study in the *Light-Fire (Agni) Yoga* methods taught by Russell Schofield and associates in the School of Actualism. I came to recognize these methods, which I still practice and use in my healing and teaching work, to be similar in many ways to those described in *Vajrayana* Buddhism, Tantra and Taoism, as well as European alchemy, as interpreted by C.G.Jung and his followers.

Shamanic journey methods are practiced worldwide in indigenous societies for purposes of healing and divination. Such a "journey" involves what in modern terms would be called an altered or non-ordinary state of consciousness, which the shamanic practitioner undertakes on behalf of the sick individual or community. The shamanic journey, like any healing procedure, begins with a formulating of questions and intentions, followed by the practitioner going into a trance, communicating with her or her spirit allies, and then returning with information or feedback for the client. The two main methods for inducing the shamanic journey trance are hallucinogenic plants or fungi, more commonly used in the tropical and sub-tropical regions; and rhythmic drumming or rattling, more often used in the Northern Hemisphere regions of Asia, Europe and America. It has been theorized that the rhythmic pulsing induces synchronized entrainment of brain-waves, as well as heart-beat and breath-rate, and that this makes the individual more receptive to sense-impressions and intuitions from non-ordinary dimensions of reality.

I have myself participated in and learned from working with the classic shamanic drumming journey method as taught by my esteemed friends and colleagues Michael Harner and Sandra Ingerman. Many shamanic journey experiences described in classic accounts, as well as in contemporary practice, deal with the after-death realms, and with relations with deceased relatives or spirits of the dead. Although shamanic journey descriptions don't seem to explicitly refer to birth experience, we can observe that the classic shamanic lower-world journey – moving downward through a narrow, sometimes hazardous tunnel and emerging into a brighter, more open landscape – is experientially resonant with the fetal journey through the birth canal.

In *hypnotic trance states,* a dissociative disconnect from awareness of ordinary time-space reality is brought about by direct or indirect suggestion of the hypnotist. The degree of absorption or immersion in interior experience can be so profound that hypnosis has been used for anesthesia in surgery and for the recovery of repressed or dissociated memories in cases of childhood abuse and other traumatic amnesias. The verbalizations of the hypnotist function as the guiding thread that leads the person into deeper degrees of absorptive trance.

With this method also, inner experiences and observations are largely shaped or framed by the pre-existing worldview, the set and the setting. For example, it is noteworthy that Milton Erickson, the American master-hypnotherapist, who performed extraordinary healings of early childhood traumas, never ventured into the realms of prenatal experience. On the other hand, in the second half of the 20th century, a number of physicians and therapists, whose work will be discussed in Chapters One and Two, began to use hypnotic regression to access birth memories as well as prenatal experience. My own understanding of this area and this methodology has been greatly deepened also through personal participation in workshops conducted by the pioneering therapists William Emerson and Ray Castellino.

Other practitioners, working with hypnotic trance methods to track the origins of present life problems, have found themselves discovering apparent memories of past lives in different times and places, as well as experiences of the discarnate life of the soul after death. Therapists working with past-life and inter-life memories in their clients, have made these discoveries in the course of their healing work, which has often lead them to a much deeper appreciation for the mysteries of death, re-birth and *karma*. From the point of view of the healing practitioner the purpose of such work is to find resolution to painful problems or conflicts – not to prove the validity of any particular doctrines or beliefs.

I should point out however that an acceptance of the actuality of reincarnation is a near-universal in the world's religions and spiritual teachings outside of the West. It was part of Christ's teaching as well, before being expunged from Church doctrine in the early centuries of the Christian era. It was declared incompatible with the Christian core doctrine of salvation of the faithful after death – an ideological maneuver that vastly increased the Church's power and wealth, by emphasizing faith over individual choice.

In my own work I have found that getting in touch with soul memories of prenatal, past-life or inter-life experience can bring about deeply healing changes in a person's psyche. This is a form of validation that is in accord with the basic principle of empirical medicine – that the proof of the diagnosis and the correctness of the remedy lies in the cure. Winafred Lucas, Ph.D (1911-2006) a wise psychologist who compiled a useful compendium of hypnotic regression methods, was an invaluable mentor for me in exploring these methods and areas.

Breathing practices provide another method of inducing profoundly altered states of consciousness in which pre-natal, post-mortem and transpersonal experiences of various kinds may be accessed. Controlled breathing methods known as *pranayama* are an essential part of the disciplines of yoga, functioning to coordinate and harmonize the relations between body and mind. Andrew Weil, MD, in his expositions of integrative medicine, has called breath "the master key to healing." In Buddhist mindfulness meditation *(vipassana)*, the non-analytical, non-judgmental observing of the currents of breath is a basic practice, preparatory to the more difficult mindfulness in relation to feelings, sensations and the stream of thoughts. Therapists working to heal imprints from birth and pre-birth experience, both on dry land and in water, have developed a variety of breathing practices that facilitate conscious regression. I have myself participated in a number of such birth-related breathwork sessions with several different practicioners, gaining valuable insights.

The most comprehensive use of breathing as an avenue to non-ordinary states and realms of consciousness is the *holotropic breathwork* developed by Stanislav and Christina Grof, who are also my long-term friends and collaborators. In this form of group work, intensive hyperventilation is accompanied by dramatic music and focused bodywork. The dissociative element in such states can be quite significant. In one holotropic breathwork session, my sitting partner informed me afterwards that while I was doing the breathing, I at one point sat up and spoke words in a language she neither understood nor recognized – and I myself had absolutely zero recall of this event.

In this book I will be drawing on descriptions of experiences from all these sources, as well as my own experiences ("first-person empiricism") and those of individuals with whom I have worked in my psychotherapy and alchemical divination work, using shamanic, yogic and hypnotic regression methods, both with and without perceptual amplification through psychedelics.

I want to emphasize, as stated above, that the conscious recall of prenatal (or other-world) experiences in such states is not a pharmacological drug effect, any more than recall with hypnotic regression is an effect of hypnosis, or shamanic drumming journey visions are an effect of the drumming. Psychedelic, hypnotic, drumming or breathing techniques can facilitate dissolving the barriers of amnesia and amplify perception – but the individual's intention/question and the context provided by the guide or therapist are the key determinants of the healing process and the insights associated with it.

In Chapter One, *Birth – Traumatic Realities, Ecstatic Potentials*, I describe the work of Stanislav Grof and others on how the experience of traumatic birth can permanently affect the deep structure of the psyche; how adults can remember the subjective experience of being born; and how the fetus during birth is exquisitely attuned to the feelings and thoughts of their parents and the social environment of their family. I suggest a simple and revealing *divination to your first response on being born*. I describe the work of the psychohistory researchers, which has revealed disturbing but important correlations between traumatic birth and the collective pathologies of violence and war; and the work of water birth pioneers in the US and in Russia, who have demonstrated that spiritually-based birthing practices may replace the usually anticipated anxiety and pain of birthing with ecstatic, even orgasmic experiences.

In Chapter Two, *Prenatal Imprints and Ancestral Connections*, I relate how hypnotic regressions of adults to their pre-natal experience demonstrate deep and perceptive awareness of family life events and subjective states. Through intentional empathic connection adults can tune in to their mother's and father's states of mind during the prenatal period and this can have profoundly healing effects. This chapter includes a *divination to the parental imprints at conception*. In dreams, visions and divinations, adults and children may relate impressions and messages from souls choosing to incarnate into their family – clearly beyond any possible memory from biological life. I relate findings from the divinations to connect and reconcile with one's ancestors – and the deep peace of mind and sense of purpose that can result from such connections.

In Chapter Three, *Death and the Hereafter,* I consider the paradoxical analogy between the experience of dying and the experience of being born: both are expansions of consciousness into unknown realms of being. I discuss the cross-cultural tradition of a three-day transition period or wake, in which the soul orients itself to its new out-of-body existence; the distinction between near-death and ego-death experiences; and new and ancient ways of preparing for dying, including those involving psychedelics. I describe some ancient myths of guides and guardians of the land of the dead, and the Tibetan Buddhist teachings on dying and the initial *bardo* states. This chapter includes a *divination to your dying day* – as a demonstration of how such a meditative practice can significantly decrease our usual anxiety about death.

In Chapter Four, *Life Between Lives,* I discuss the revelations from NDEs (near-death experiences), which have afforded unparalleled access to the after-life realms; as well as from communications between the living and the spirits of the dead, both direct and those mediated by others. I discuss the after-death teachings of ancient Egypt, particularly in relation to the notion of the life-review; and the Tibetan Buddhist teachings of heavenly and hellish *bardo* visions. And I describe divination journeys to the council of ancestral souls, and some of the remarkable teachings and findings from these journeys.

In Chapter Five, *From Incarnation to Conception and Rebirth*, I chart the journeys of the soul through the after-death realms on the pathways to a new life, drawing on the Tibetan Buddhist *bardo of rebirth* teachings and our divinations to the council of guiding spirits, which stands behind or mingled with the ancestral council. I also relate the beautiful stories from the Jewish *midrashim* of the Angel Lailah, known as the "midwife of souls," who escorts and guides the incarnating souls into their new conception and rebirth.

In presenting this work for publication, I want to express my gratitude and appreciation to the students, colleagues and friends with whom I have had the privilege of exploring the realms beyond birth and death; to the pioneering doctors, healers and scientists whose work has expanded and deepened our understanding of these realms; and, above all, to the spiritual teachers and ascended masters who painstakingly and tirelessly guide our spiritual evolution on this troubled Earth.

One

Birth – Traumatic Realities, Ecstatic Potentials

I wish to examine the role and significance of birth and the prenatal epoch in human psychological life and present a model for understanding perinatal ("birth-related") and prenatal formative influences on human development. My understanding of this area has been significantly influenced by the ground-breaking research and theorizing of the Czech-born psychiatrist Stanislav Grof, whose work in psycholytic psychotherapy with LSD led him to study the impact of birth patterns on psychopathology and subsequent transpersonal experiences, and demonstrated how transformative realizations can emerge out of crisis experiences when birth patterns are taken into account.

Grof's central theoretical contribution is the identification of a four-fold sequence of "basic perinatal matrices" (BPMs), and the impact of these patterns in psychedelic and other non-ordinary states of consciousness. In the 1970s, when I came across Grof's writings on perinatal experiences with psychedelics, they were a revelation for me: for the first time I felt I understood certain aspects of psychedelic experiences I had had years before, in my studies as part of the Harvard psilocybin project, particularly some painful, hellish visions I had never been able to interpret before.

My colleagues and I at Harvard had learned early on that Freud's psychoanalytic theories clearly did not touch the psychedelic realms. Jung's writings were more helpful in accommodating the mythic and mystical dimensions of psychedelic experiences, but did not explain the extreme and violent nature of some of the hellish bad trips. In the model based on *The Tibetan Book of the Dead*, the Buddhist teachings of three *bardo* stages one goes through between death and rebirth was metaphysically illuminating, but did not really describe the typical course of a psychedelic experience.

I had also found the theories and body-oriented therapy methods of Wilhelm Reich very apposite in helping to understand the energy-flow and energy-blockage experiences that can occur in these altered states of consciousness. Grof's model, on the other hand, gave a detailed description of the content of certain experiences -- tracing them to the qualitative template or matrix provided in one or another of the four BPMs.

Let me give a personal example. Here is my description of parts of a high-dose psilocybin session I had when we were still at Harvard:

> As I looked around the room I saw great bands of moving streams of energy particles traversing the space, passing through and between myself and the other people. We all seemed to be part of these moving, ever-changing bands of energy. They were familiar to me from other psilocybin sessions, when I had seen them as luminous vibrating filigree networks. But this time, the intensity frightened me. As my fear-level increased, the energy bands congealed and stopped moving; they took on a greyish hue, like prison bars. All at once I felt immobilized and trapped, like a fly in a gigantic metallic spiders's web. I couldn't even talk and explain what was happening to me; my voice felt paralyzed. Everyone seemed to be frozen into immobility by these metallic web-cages. I felt my mind was paralyzed too. I couldn't think or understand what was happening. I couldn't tell whether what I was experiencing was real or a drug-induced hallucination (an experience psychiatry refers to as "derealization"). I felt completely de-humanized, not even like a biological organism, more like a mechanical puppet or device (from *Birth of a Psychedelic Culture*, p. 30-34).

The following are Grof's descriptions of typical LSD experiences from the perinatal realm of BPM II, the stage of the birth process when contractions have started, but the cervix has not yet opened, so that no movement is possible for the fetus.

> The activation of this matrix results in a rather characteristic spiritual experience of "no exit" or "hell." The subject feels encaged in a claustrophobic world ... This experience is characterized by a striking darkness of the visual field and by ominous colors. ... Another typical category of visions related to this perinatal matrix involves the dehumanized, grotesque, and bizarre world of automata, robots and mechanical gadgets... or of a meaningless "honky tonk" or "cardboard" world. Agonizing feelings of separation, alienation, metaphysical loneliness, helplessness, hopelessness, inferiority and guilt are standard components of BPM II. ... An interesting variety of the second perinatal matrix seems to be related to the very onset and the initial stages of the delivery. This situation is experienced in LSD sessions as an increasing awareness of an imminent and vital danger or as cosmic engulfment.... intensification of this experience typically results in the vision of a gigantic and irresistible whirlpool, a cosmic maelstrom sucking the subject and his world relentlessly to its center. ...typical symptoms involve extreme pressures on the head and body. (Grof, S. *Realms of the Human Unconscious*, p. 115-121).

I understood then how in such experiences, complexes of thoughts, images and feelings are conflated with memories of extreme bodily sensations from the corresponding stage of the birth process. In another session with psilocybin, I was triggered by a chance interaction with a friend into feeling guilty about something I had said. Next, I found myself in a medieval torture dungeon, where I was being beaten to a bloody pulp by men with gigantic clubs. While the experience of guilt was explicable in terms of the interpersonal dynamics, the grotesque, torturous intensity of these hellish visions was not. Here is what Grof says about the dynamics of BPM III, where the cervix has opened, and now there is movement – intense, powerful pushing and thrusting.

> The most important characteristic of this pattern is the atmosphere of a titanic struggle, frequently attaining catastrophic proportions. The intensity of painful tension reaches a degree that appears far beyond what any human can bear. … sadomasochistic orgies…unbridled murderous aggression… tortures and cruelties of all kinds, mutilations and self-mutilations. (Grof, S. *op. cit.* p. 123-124).

Having observed hundreds of birth-related sessions in individuals and groups, with psychedelic as well as other forms of activation and amplification, I can attest that such experiences typical of BPM stages II and III can be readily identified by an observer, even if the subjects themselves do not initially make such identification with birth memories. The objective facts of one's birth, if available, can then often be correlated with the qualitative subjective experience. For example, a person who on a psychedelic journey experiences extreme tension and choking sensation around the throat, may find that this is connected to the cord having been wrapped around the neck during delivery. Or the person may breathe laboriously and vigorously, while asserting that there is "not enough air," and "I've got to get outside." Or there may be continuous squirming, twisting, rolling and leg pushing movements, accompanied by subjective feelings of struggle and exhausting effort.

Grof's model of the birthing process and the four perinatal matrices can accommodate both positive and negative experiences, and recollections of experiences, in each phase. The experience of BPM I, the intra-uterine floating oneness in the womb, before labor contractions start, can be experienced as the "oceanic feeling" that Sigmund Freud had described; but it can also be, in the case of mothers whose womb was toxic with infection, alcohol or narcotics, like floating in a noxious swamp. BPM II can be experienced as unbearable pressure and constriction, or as the calm and patient endurance of immobility. BPM III can be violently explosive aggression and/or powerful, arousing sexuality. BPM IV, the release from the womb, can be a vertiginous falling, or the ecstatic release of flying.

In his writings on the birth matrices Grof has pointed out that he was, in a sense, reviving the long-neglected theories of Otto Rank (1884-1939), one of Freud's closest disciples, who wrote of the trauma of birth as an important source of anxiety-laden memories and fantasies in the unconscious. Rank had suggested, in his book *The Myth of the Birth of the Hero*, that world mythology contains numerous stories that reflect aspects of the birth experience. The pioneering prenatal regression therapist William Emerson and his collaborators, in their book *Remembering Our Home*, have pointed to the parallels between the story of the birth of Jesus and the archetypal journey of the soul from pre-conception to birth.

Another psychoanalytic theorist who incorporated aspects of birth into his thinking is Henry A. Murray (1893-1988), the inventor of the projective *Thematic Apperception Test (TAT)*, who was a student of both Freud and Jung, and who taught at Harvard during the time of the Psilocybin Project (he was one of my professors there). Based on his analysis of fantasy productions of "normal" people, as well as neurotic patients, Murray found a cluster of themes of feeling enclosed, shut in, pressed down or imprisoned, which he named a *claustral complex*, and related explicitly to intra-uterine experience. This complex is clearly identical to what Grof calls the second basic perinatal matrix (BPM II).

Breath-related methods of accessing birth memories were developed independently by therapists in a lineage called *Rebirthing*, described in books by Leonard Orr and Sondra Ray.

In this approach, one uses continuous or circular breathing, without holding the breath, while being supported in a warm water environment by the therapist. I have myself undergone several series of sessions, with different therapists using this method, with great benefit in terms of lessened interior somatic tensions.

> I remember in one such warm water session, floating face down with a snorkel, I kept bumping with my head against the wall of the tub – the totally unconscious, bodily momentum reproducing the head-first movement down the birth-canal. I also remember, in another rebirthing session, suddenly encountering a wall of death-terror – from which I instinctively recoiled and would have bolted, if the therapist holding me had not been able to assure me through her touch, that this was a passing panic that I would survive, just as I had survived my actual birth.

Writings by David Chamberlain, Thomas Verny and others have gathered and presented copious evidence that both adults (in trance regression) and very young children (in spontaneous relaxed moods) can remember details of the birth process and of intra-uterine existence. In order to be verbalized and shared, these pre-verbal, somatic memory experiences are translated in some way. Toddlers may talk of being in water, or swimming, of coming through a tunnel, and of hearing a rhythmic sound, like "poon-poon" – likely the maternal heart-beat.

One young girl said that when she was in her mother's tummy, "there was a snake in there with me," an obvious reference to the umbilical cord. She also said there was a "doggie in there" that she played with and that barked. The mother confirmed that the family acquired a puppy when she was five months pregnant and the puppy would lie on her belly during the latter part of the pregnancy.

Perinatal regressions have revealed what sensitive parents and birth attendants also know – that newborns are wise, knowing beings who understand what's happening and are exquisitely attuned to the emotional state and motivations of those around them. They are often frustrated because they can't make their bodies and limbs work and feel overwhelmed at the intensity of the sensory input – light, cold, loud noises, rough textures – which are such a marked contrast to the pre-birth environment. The potential traumas of birth, especially under the heavily mechanical, sterile conditions of modern hospitals are well recognized. William Emerson has estimated that up to 60% of all births in modern America are traumatic for the neonate. The impact of pre- and perinatal shock and trauma is every bit as important, if not more so, than trauma in subsequent infancy and childhood.

Conversely, the resolution of perinatal and prenatal traumas can facilitate and accelerate the resolution of later neurotic and character disorders. The reason for this is clear – the armoring constrictions originating in prenatal experience are more deep-seated than those stemming from later experiences in childhood and beyond. These armorings exist not only in the as yet undeveloped exterior musculature of the torso and limbs, but are embedded in the interior tissues and impact the functioning of the autonomic or vegetative nervous system.

Practitioners of the holotropic breathwork developed by Grof have found that working with peri-natal (birth-related) experiences can produce not only resolution of deep-seated neurotic and psychosomatic pathologies, but also heightened access to previously unimagined realms of transpersonal spiritual experiences. Such findings support the notion that while floating in the watery environment of the womb, the fetal soul is exquisitely sensitive to the mother's emotional state and is also not so far removed yet from its spiritual home in the Divine world.

The imprinted body-memories of birth, which are often painful to the point of trauma, when resolved can open the doorways to the heavenly or spiritual realms from which our souls begin their earthly journey into incarnation. Something like this may be the meaning behind the mysterious and evocative dialogue between the Master Jesus and the sceptical scholar-priest Nicodemus:

> Jesus said, "Truly, truly, I say to you, unless a man is born again, he cannot see the kingdom of God."
>
> Nicodemus said to him, "How can an old man be born again? Can he enter again a second time into his mother's womb and be born?"
>
> Jesus answered, saying to him, "Truly, truly, I say to you, Unless a man is born of water and the Spirit, he cannot enter into the kingdom of God.
>
> What is born of flesh is flesh; what is born of Spirit is spirit."
>
> *(John 3:3-6)*

Physical, psychological and social factors affecting birth

Strikingly different birth experiences, and subsequent characteristic attitudes, are reported by the Caesarean-born. I once heard a television comedian who told how his Caesarean birth predisposed him to prefer to exit from rooms through the window rather than the door, like everyone else. Jane English, in her book *Different Doorway,* has related her own experiences and interviews with others who have come into the world in this way. English reported finding a characteristic trait of frustrated efficacy that seemed to be connected to this primal experience of not being permitted to push their way through to freedom. Re-birthing therapy with conscious awareness of such primal imprints can then help to release them.

An impact somewhat similar to the frustrated efficacy of Caesarean birth is often reported when adults relive the experience of the mother being anesthetized at birth. I have observed in my own perinatal regressions a sense of the dynamic process of pushing, being "flat-lined" or numbed-out at a certain point. Obviously, the mother's anesthesia numbs the baby as well. Such observations are among prime considerations behind the natural birth movement, in which preparation and conscious assisted breathing, active birthing positions and possibly a warm water environment can mitigate pain and empower both the mother and the infant.

William Emerson and his colleagues have also been able to identify with remarkable precision the effects of the mother's pelvic structure and the positioning of the baby's head on the physiognomy of the face. Whichever side of the face is lying down is being pushed over the bony protrusion of the tail-bone, which often leads to marked displacement of facial musculature. Having once observed this effect in myself and others during an Emerson workshop, it is an easy matter when looking at a photograph of someone's adult face to recognize which side they were lying on during birth. Where there was a comfortable fit between maternal pelvic and infant cranial size, the face is perfectly symmetrical.

A mismatch between the *gender expectations* and hopes of one or both of the parents and the unborn's recognition of its gender can have life-long consequences for the personality style and attitudes of the individual. Such a mismatch can even affect the birthing process itself and can be resolved if the parents are sensitive to it.

David Chamberlain relates the story of a woman whose pregnancy at term threatened to require a forceps intervention, because her fetus had not turned. Knowing about conscious communication with the unborn and having practiced it, she meditatively attuned herself to her child, asking what was blocking the birthing process. The fetus's telepathic responsive was clear – "You're hoping for a girl and I'm a boy." Realizing this was no time for dissimulation, the mother replied – "yes, it's true, I was hoping for a girl. But please know I promise to love and cherish you with all my heart, whether boy or girl." Two hours later, the fetus turned spontaneously, without medical assistance.

The evidence from reports by children and adults regressed to perinatal experience, overwhelmingly supports the principle that babies in the womb are acutely attuned to their mother's body sensations, memories and emotions, as well as thoughts and beliefs. Indeed, how could it be otherwise? Mother and fetus are inhabiting the same body, with the same blood circulating, and are thus intrinsically identical. A woman in one of my groups reported that, during a birth regression session, she felt cold fear while in the womb. She was able to identify the fear as caused by her mother's near-fatal birthing of her previous child. Through conscious therapeutic regression such unconscious identifications can be brought into awareness and either let go completely, or transformed into empathic understanding. If not recognized and processed through, they can remain as life-long emotional undercurrents.

> Only recently, when I was already in my sixties, after decades of personal work in this area, I was able to track my life-long body-sensation of bloated fullness, to the feeling my mother had when she was pregnant with me. This was a maternal body-image, taken on by the fetus, and retained (unconsciously) by the adult for the better part of a life-time. It goes without saying that to release it was liberating and did not require a rejection of my affectional bond with my (long deceased) mother.

Under ordinary conditions, these are unconscious identifications: the fetus (and later the newborn child) assumes the mother's emotional states by sympathetic resonance. Parental conflicts or separation during the prenatal and birth period can have life-long impacts, especially when a parent is not truthful (whether through trauma or malice) to their children about the fate of the other parent.

> A woman's father died in an accident a few months after the daughter was born. Her mother, in shock, never told her anything about her father. In her mind, she had been abandoned by him. The mother, traumatized by the near-simultaneous violent death of her husband and birth of her daughter, never recovered. She became neglectful of her children and alcoholic, and sent her daughter to an orphanage school at age four. When this woman got pregnant with a son in her early twenties, she was repeating her mother's pattern of early marriage and pregnancy.
>
> In a reconciliation divination with her mother and maternal ancestors, she moved from a place of bitterness and anger to a place of peace and compassion. In a reconciliation divination with her father, she expressed gratitude for receiving the thread of life from him and his ancestors. She ceased to blame him for "abandoning" her, realizing she had adopted this belief as a child in the absence of any true communication about his fate or his life.

Parental separation for whatever reason, at or near the time of birth, leading to the child's being raised by grandparents or adopted outside the family – can leave a life-long, haunting feeling of not being wanted. It can also result in an almost mythic quest to at least see or communicate, if only once, with one's "true" genetic parents. Fortunately, in recent times adoption agencies in the US have started to reverse the long-standing practice of keeping the original birth-parents' identity from the child and so-called "open adoptions" are becoming more common.

A man in one of my groups reported becoming aware of how the basic soul agreement between the parents was ruptured at birth.

> What came through very strongly for me was during the prenatal period and after birth an agreement was broken between my mother and father. And I was able to see in the course of my life how I was sort of playing that role out of breaking agreements…My mother was completely in love with my father…she was quite young…and there was a beautiful moment, in the divination, seeing them together. He was a musician, he played with a steel band and they would travel. And he broke the (soul) agreement – upon my birth…he left her. And she was devastated.

Further along in the divination, meeting with the council of ancestral souls, this man could recognize that at that level of soul there was no rupture nor devastation – just the working out of karmic lessons.

Similarly, a woman physician experienced, during a perinatal regression, how she and her mother were fatefully entwined – but her soul's life-purpose was beyond that fixation.

> Reliving my birth experience I'm experiencing unbearable breathing difficulty, perhaps related to the caul (*caput galeatum*) I was born with. When I attempt to relive looking into my mother's eyes at birth, it takes a long time – her eyes don't seem to be looking at me, but through me. I'm reading her face and know that she knows that our fates are somehow conjoined. I get this message… In this life you should stop looking at your mother and instead look to your destiny. This message comforts me and makes perfect sense.

Our personality can make choices that are not in accord with the soul vision and agreement. This is the principle of free will: the Spirit guides – but does not impose. The basic agreement between three souls, to conceive and give birth to a child, may be kept – but the personalities involved may lose it, may forget, or may not be able to live up to this agreement. It happens all the time. People with children, unborn or born, get divorced, are separated by war or accident, get addicted and distracted, commit crimes, go to jail. Nevertheless, the basic agreement between the parental souls is the starting point of our earthly existence and tuning into it with compassion and gratitude can be immensely liberating.

> **Divination to your First Response at Birth**
>
> *The following practice can yield valuable insights into core themes of one's life. Though most adults would claim not to remember anything about their birth, a brief attunement and inner questioning may yield an insightful answer, which the verbal centers in the brain can translate into adult words, just as you translate non-verbal dream imagery. After entering into a meditative space and attuning yourself especially to your mother's and father's spirit – ask yourself what was your first response, your first thought, feeling or attitude toward the world on being born?*

A schizophrenic man I was working with, some years ago, when I asked him this question, immediately said – "I wanted to say to my parents – I'm sorry for causing you so much trouble." This apologetic feeling of guilt at causing trouble to his parents remained as an emotional undercurrent throughout his adult life.

My own response to this self-questioning divination was to realize that my first attitude was ambivalent: part of me was excited by the adventure of being in the world, and part of me was anxious, worrying about whether I would be safe. I could see how this kind of basic ambivalence has been a core theme throughout most of my life. Only in my later years, past the age of fifty, have I come to release the anxiety with the recognition that, of course, the world was not safe, and to practice equanimity with that thought. This was the realization of "the wisdom of insecurity," as Alan Watts, who was one of my teachers, called it in his book of that title. Existence inevitably involves suffering, as the Buddhists say.

Traumatic Birth and Collective Psychopathology

In his studies of perinatal imagery, whether triggered by LSD or by holotropic breathwork, Stanislav Grof was struck by the connection of birth trauma to collective expressions of violence and destructiveness.

> ...the reliving of birth in various forms of experiential psychotherapy involves not only concrete replay of the original emotions and sensations, but is typically associated with a variety of experiences from the collective unconscious portraying scenes of unimaginable violence. Among these are often powerful sequences depicting wars, revolutions, racial riots, concentration camps, totalitarianism, and genocide...The spontaneous emergence of this imagery during the reliving of birth is often associated with convincing insights concerning perinatal origin of such extreme forms of human violence (Grof, S. *The Psychology of the Future*, p. 302).

Working with completely different methods – the analysis of fantasy imagery in historical documents, media reports, political tracts and cartoons – Lloyd DeMause and his psychohistory colleagues have found striking correlations of fetal and perinatal imagery with wars and mass violence. DeMause's books – *The Foundations of Psychohistory, The Emotional Life of Nations* – and articles in the *Journal of Psychohistory*, while focused on historical and cross-cultural patterns of child abuse and violence toward children, have also included fantasy material relating to birth and pre-natal life.

> I wish to present...the evidence which has led me to the following three conclusions: 1. That mental life begins in the womb with a fetal drama which is remembered and elaborated upon by later childhood events; 2. that this fetal drama is the basis for the history and culture of each age, as modified by evolving child-rearing styles; and 3. that the fetal drama is traumatic, so it must be repeated endlessly in cycles of dying and rebirth, as expressed in group-fantasies which even today continue to determine much of our national political life (DeMause, 1982).

In his psychohistorical analyses of political propaganda during the run-up period prior to a war, DeMause observed that "wars are from their beginning experienced as direct repetition of the birth struggle, begun when nations are 'smothered and unable to draw a breath,' continuing until they can 'see the light at the end of the tunnel' and even 'aborted' if ended too soon."

One of Hitler's favorite *memes*, that he used to inspire ordinary Germans for his territorial push Eastward, was that the German people needed a larger *Lebensraum* ("living space") - a typical thought for the fetus struggling through the constrictive conditions of the birth canal at term. The dropping of bombs is also associated with the birth process. Even the dropping of the nuclear bomb on Hiroshima was seen as a birthing ritual: The bomb was nicknamed "Little Boy" and dropped from the belly of a plane named after the pilot's mother. When it was dropped, General Groves cabled President Truman that, "The baby was born."

This line of work confirms the profound impact of perinatal factors not only on individual development, but on the collective behavior of groups, tribes and nations and indeed, one could say, the fate of human civilization. These conclusions, arrived at by entirely different methods, also emphasize the need for reform of birthing practices, as argued by many pioneering obstetricians, midwives and child advocates, based on their work with individuals and families.

Under the influence of visionary obstetricians like Frederick Leboyer, Michel Odent and others, gentler, more conscious birthing practices and environments have found a place in the West. Such practices have functioned to humanize the birthing process, taking it out of the category of an illness to be treated in a hospital by medical technology, and instead recognizing it as an innate human process, guided by instinct, empathy and Spirit, to be facilitated and protected.

Water birthing and ecstatic/orgasmic birthing

Painlessly, even ecstatically, birthing in a water environment may be both a recollection of our evolutionary ancestry as aquatic primates and an anticipation of our evolutionary potentials. The theory, propounded by Elaine Morgan and others, that the evolutionary transition from arboreal anthropoid primates to upright walking humanoids occurred in the wetlands environments (swamps, marshes, seashores) of East Africa three to four million years ago, is dismissed by mainstream paleontology. Nevertheless is has some very convincing evidence and proponents, including Michel Odent, the renowned French obstetrician and pioneer of birthing in a watery environment.

Birthing in water has been a core element of the practices of a collective of parents and midwives/educators in Russia, who challenged the medical establishments contention that birthing in water was dangerous. The danger of birth complications is eliminated or greatly reduced, when the mother is assisted throughout her pregnancy (or even before) to work through her own residual birth trauma, in group processes involving counseling, stretching and breathing yoga, couples work and expressive art.

With such intensive preparation over the prenatal period, involving also a spiritual and religious component, guided as requested by Orthodox priests – the collective organized birthing camps on the Black Sea, in the Summer months. Here the mothers and soon-to-be mothers, attending midwives, fathers and children, swam with dolphins and gathered to celebrate the arrival of the newborns. Under such conditions births may be not only not painful, but ecstatic, even orgasmic for the mother, and at any rate a welcoming of the infant into a loving, spiritually awake family and community.

The possibility of the birthing experience being orgasmic for the mother may seem far removed from the usual cultural expectations about the inevitable painfulness of birth. But there is other evidence that it may be more common than we realize. Both birthing and orgasm involve intense rhythmic pulsations of contraction-relaxation of the interior pelvic musculature. A friend of mine in Germany told me that during an ayahuasca experience he relived his birth from both his own and his mother's perspective. He realized that his mother's experience was orgasmic and when he told her about this, she confirmed it, though at first slightly embarrassed and perplexed as to how her son could know.

During a session of rebirthing regression amplified by a short-acting tryptamine (*5-methoxy-DMT*) a woman reported re-experiencing simultaneously her own birth and her experience of birthing her child – and orgasm. The pelvic contraction-relaxation pulsations were somehow overlayed or interlayed with the sensation-memories of these core experiences of her life. Some might be tempted to attribute this fused reliving of birthing and being born to the effect of the psychedelic substance. However, the pioneering researchers Stanislav and Christina Grof have demonstrated that such fused experiences occur quite frequently in their holotropic breathwork sessions, without any drugs. In fact in their recent book *Holotropic Breathwork*, there is a reproduction of a painting (*illustration #4g*) done by a woman, of just such an experience during a breathwork session.

In their recognition and explicit honoring of the spiritual or transpersonal essence of the processes and relations involved in birth, the Russian waterbirth collective goes far beyond what has been attempted in the West. An amazing film documenting this community and their practices, *Birth Into Being,* has been made by Elena Vladimirova and her colleagues. When you see the midwife Tatiana Sargunas giving birth to her third child, with her other two children watching, squatting with total body relaxation in a transparent warm-water tank, with her open, calmly smiling face looking at the cameraman/father, while reaching between her open legs with one hand, and easing the neonate into the water-earth – without so much as a flicker of discomfort; and then you see the babies and children born in this way, swimming fearlessly underwater and above, and around playful dolphins, you can't help but feel that this is a new evolutionary generation coming into Earth.

I have sometimes thought that perhaps the Russian waterbirth collective, and others who have developed methods of ecstatic, spiritual birthing have managed to start unraveling what I call the *curse of Yahweh*. In the *Book of Genesis*, that fountainhead of Western religious ideology, the Lord Yahweh delivers a triple curse on the new humans who have just been created. He curses the serpent, the Earth and the woman – "in pain you shall bring forth children." Is not the association of birthing with pain here being given an ideological justification? Perhaps, and hopefully, in the water-born children and others of similar disposition, the violence gene can be maneuvered into recessive dormancy.

These children, born with full parental recognition and support of their spiritual essence and divine heritage, with or without a watery environment, are children who will not be easily manipulated by threats, or deceived by dishonesty. They seem to know they are sovereign souls, equal to all other souls and deserving of recognition and respect, even in the infant and child phase of their life when they are physically completely dependent on parental care and support. Like children who are consciously conceived, that Emerson has described, and like the children with indigo-colored auras that some educators have described, they know they have equal access to Source Spirit and have trust in their ability to learn, to grow and to unfold their soul potentials.

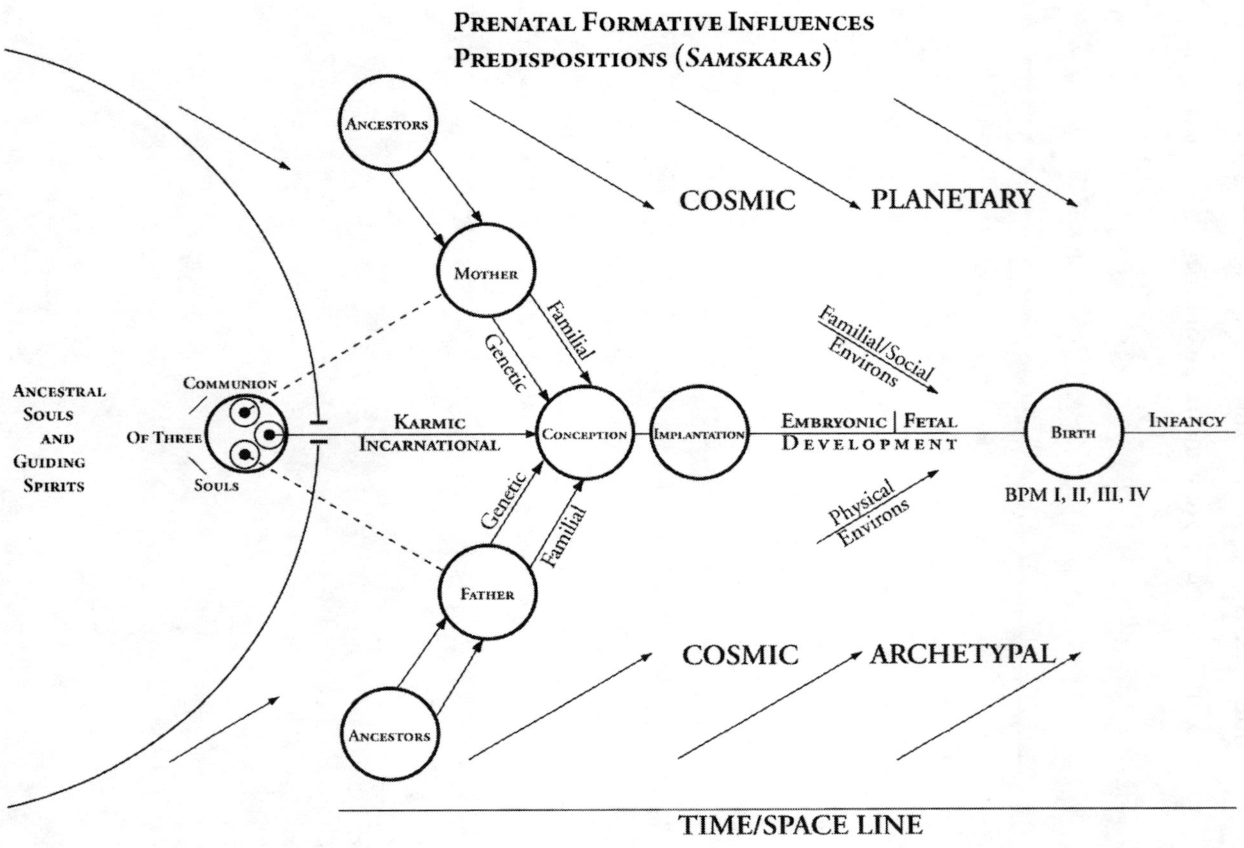
Prenatal Formative Influences
Predispositions (Samskaras)
Ancestors
Mother
Father
Ancestors
Cosmic
Planetary
Cosmic
Archetypal
Ancestral Souls and Guiding Spirits
Communion Of Three Souls
Karmic Incarnational
Genetic
Familial
Genetic
Familial
Conception
Implantation
Embryonic | Fetal
Development
Familial/Social Environs
Physical Environs
Birth
BPM I, II, III, IV
Infancy
TIME/SPACE LINE

A summary overview of what we have learned from pre- and perinatal psychology, as well as traditional esoteric teachings, about the prenatal period is shown in the chart. *Samskaras* (from *sam* "together" and *kri* "make") are associative imprints, markings, tracks or traces, that predispose us to think, feel and perceive in particular ways. For example, genetic predispositions to certain illnesses and personality weaknesses are *samskaras*. But there may also be, in some individuals, *samskaras* of genetic resilience, innate resistance to certain diseases or character strengths and health.

There are also familial, ancestral, religious and ethnic predispositions – traditions, attitudes, talents, interests and gifts. These are the habits of thought and action that are passed on by grandparents, aunts and uncles, as well as parents – for example when they say to the child "in our family, we always…" In my alchemical divination training, one of the divinations that I teach is called *reconnecting and reconciling with the ancestors*. In the next chapter, I will discuss the observations and discoveries that can result when people intentionally tune in with their ancestral lineages and the associated gifts and challenges. The chart also shows how *physical environmental factors* (e.g. climate, health of the mother), *social factors* (e.g. the family's presence in war or in poverty), and *familial factors* (e.g. the father's leaving, or a grandparent dying) can play a significant role in affecting prenatal development and the birth process itself.

In the ancient divinatory art of astrology, the positions of the planets in our solar system and the geometric angles between them at birth are seen as important symbolic indicators of the life challenges and opportunities to come. One could argue that if we concede that environmental factors of climate and local ecosystem health are influential in infancy, birth and prenatal life, then it is no great stretch to imagine that the current positions and angular relations of the other planets in our Solar System may also be affecting life and consciousness on Earth. Our home planet Earth is, after all, embedded in the complex, ever-changing gravitational and electro-magnetic fields of the entire Solar System.

Two

Prenatal Imprints and Ancestral Connections

Psychological studies of the perceptions, feelings, thoughts and communication abilities of the pre-born child, as reported in works by Thomas Verny, David Chamberlain and others, have revealed a vast world of prenatal experience every bit as rich and differentiated as the experiential world of the neonate and infant. In hypnotherapeutic regression trances, adults have reported details of conversations and events in the familial and social environment while they were *in utero*. The following two examples are from David Chamberlain's writings:

> A woman whose mother was a concert cellist could trace her ecstatic response to Bach's cello partitas to her mother's playing of them when she was pregnant.

> A man tracked his peculiar negative visceral reaction to Buick automobiles to his father's statement, on learning of his wife's pregnancy, that "darn, we won't be able to afford the Buick now that I've always wanted."

The mother's emotional state during the pregnancy is completely absorbed by the fetus she is carrying inside of her, and experienced with total identification. During a prenatal regression with mild psychedelic amplification and yoga *asanas*, a woman in one of my workshops reported –

> Changing my position to the child posture brought me immediately into the prenatal phase. In my mother's womb I am experiencing feeling cold, not safe, lonely and afraid. I recognize these as my mother's feelings. I sense being unwanted – my mother almost died at the birth of my brother. I'm aware that my father wanted another boy – feel sadness about this and see suddenly how I rejected my girl-ness as being not alright. I see how because of this I tried to act more like a boy when growing up, including taking on the smoking habit.

While therapeutic interventions naturally tend to focus on uncovering and releasing the roots of dysfunctional and distressing patterns, clearly healthy and positive emotional states are absorbed as well. When the maternal and larger familial emotional climate is one of joyous anticipation and delight at the arrival of the new soul – the stage is set for a life-long basic optimism and *joie-de-vivre*.

Not only the mother's but also the father's psychic state and that of other family members, such as siblings and grandparents, are also registered by the pre-born child. Parental or familial tensions and conflicts during the prenatal phase can have significant impacts on the fetal psyche and subsequent character. The fetus is likely to assume that he/she is the cause of the conflict between the parents, just as it is well-known that young children will take responsibility for familial conflicts on themselves.

The thought of regret over the pregnancy, or even the passing thought of terminating it, can leave deep-seated feelings of being unwanted in the prenatal fetus. Actual attempts at abortion can have devastating traumatic effects. The Australian psychiatrist Graham Farrant (1933-1993), one of the pioneers of prenatal regression, has reported, in his publications, how he confirmed with his mother his subjective fetal memory of an abortion attempt that nearly succeeded in killing him – though he subsequently healed this murderous wound.

Therapists and healers working in this troubling (and politically charged) field have developed approaches for healing the after-effects of abortion attempts in the child who is born, and the residual guilt and shame on the part of women (and their partners) who completed an abortion. Knowing what we now know about the sensitivity and communicative capacities of the unborn, parents have realized that they can share their concerns with their unborn child and ask and receive forgiveness from the soul for aborting a vehicle for which they were ill prepared, or where the vehicle itself was defective. In some situations, as reported by Jane English and also observed myself, such soul-to-soul conversations have resulted in miscarriages, obviating the need for an abortion.

Parental hopes and wishes for a child of a particular gender may also play a significant role in our prenatal existence, as we have found in my groups in which we practice conscious regression to the prenatal phase, and as many prenatal therapists report. My own mother's hope for a girl as her second child, who turned out to be me, spilled over into her dressing me in girl's clothes at times during early childhood; this treatment seems to have left me with a lasting emotional resonance for the feminine human gender, perhaps even a psychological affinity with feminist social thought and Goddess spirituality.

On the other hand, I have often heard stories of women who attempted to shape their psycho-sexual development in the direction of tomboys and masculine sports, to please their father's conscious or unconscious wishes. Since the sex of the child is set at conception, gender expectations, hopes and wishes become a part of the psychic matrix in which the embryo and fetus is embedded throughout the prenatal period.

As a result of the work in this field women (and men) have become more aware of the reality of sympathetic attunement between mother and fetus during the prenatal period and have taken steps to clear up misunderstandings. A woman in one of my groups working on her childhood relationship with her parents, became aware of a disturbance in her relationship with her eight-year old son, stemming from her own anxieties, and saw how she could heal it.

> I was shown some things about my children that I need to clear up. One, with my son, he somehow feels that he can't be fully loved because he is not a girl. At one point I had made a kind of lighthearted statement, that I wouldn't know what to do with a boy and somehow, on some level, he feels that he can't be completely loved because he is not a girl. But the thing is, that I was always completely open to whichever one I had and I couldn't have been more blessed to have had a boy first. So I just really need to share that with him.

The social conditions during the prenatal period, such as war or economic depression, can influence the mother's (and father's) emotional state and therefore the fetus and child. Making the connection between the conditions of the family and the likely maternal state is sometimes sufficient to turn unconscious sympathetic identification into empathic understanding. An example, from my files of case-reports:

> A man in his sixties, suffering from long-term depression, disappointment and lack of initiative, was able to make the connection to his mother's mood during his prenatal existence. He was born in the Depression years of the 1930s and his mother's father died while she was pregnant. The mother's darkening mood of grief and despair was passed on to the fetus as a pervasive constricting body-mask, exactly the subjective equivalent to his life-long state. Tuning in with breathing and meditation, he expressed gratitude to his long-dead mother, asking for her blessing – and felt enormous release and expansion of his emotional energy-field.

A child may be conceived and born into a family where the two parents come from different, even warring, clans, classes or nations. The couple who decide to commit to love and conceive a child, in the face of larger social or familial conflict, are affirming the power and hopefulness of love and life in the face of hatred and death. It's the archetypal story of *Romeo and Juliet* and countless other loving couples in world literature and film. In our divinations to the prenatal period, we have found that in such situations, where the parents have vastly different family backgrounds, one aspect of that soul's mission may well have to do with bridging those differences.

In my work in Europe, with individuals who were conceived and born during WWII or its after-math, I have often noticed such impacts. It's the story of my parents too – my German father and British mother, raising their children in a time of war between their nations. There is a special poignancy to life-stories in which a couple from warring nations, tribes or families get married, conceive a child and then the father goes off to war. Neither parent know if he will come back alive, or wounded and traumatized. A young mother surviving the loss of her husband while pregnant may carry deep grief and/or bitterness, which is absorbed by the prenatal fetus and infant without comprehension of its origin.

Divination to the Parental Imprints at Conception

To prepare yourself, find a quiet time and place in your life and enter into a meditative space. Center awareness and identity in the Cave of the Heart, which is the whole chest cavity from the shoulders to the upper abdomen. Invoke the blessings and assistance of your guru and/or Spirit Guide(s). Ignite the purifying light-fire energy-sun in the Heart-Center and concentrate on the presence of empathy and equanimity.

To tune in to the conception event from the mother's side, turn to the left rear doorway in the Cave of the Heart. Ask to know, feel or sense – what was your mother's state of mind and heart at that time in her life? What were the family values and visions she carried for her life? How was the love that she felt toward her husband, your father? What was the sexuality like in that relationship? What were her expectations, positive and negative, about becoming pregnant, having a child, or another child, or a child of a certain gender, her wishes, hopes and fears?

Reflecting on the answers you receive to your self-divination, recognize and acknowledge that the patterns of thoughts, feelings and sensations you have identified as originating from your mother have also become part of your make-up, distinctive threads in the tapestry of your life. You can then release those threads or patterns (such as neurotic anxieties) that you took on because you had no choice, but that no longer serve your (or your mother's) life-purpose.

You can then repeat the divinatory questioning for the father's side, turning to the right rear doorway of the Cave of the Heart. You can ask the same questions about your father's state of mind and heart at the time in his life when you were first conceived and then born. An additional question you may want to ask, perhaps especially for the father's side, is – how did he feel about the state of the world, the political and economic conditions, the practical realities of work or war that might require his absence from mother and child. Here too, having identified the imprints on your psyche from the father's side, you can retain the strengths, with gratitude, and release the weaknesses, with compassion.

Milestones of the prenatal journey

As the diagram on page 30 indicates, three strands or tracks of memory imprints can be identified when regressing consciously to conception: *first*, the mother's and father's familial-genetic inheritance, genetic strengths and weaknesses; *second*, the personality, attitudes, sexual conditioning and existential orientation of each of the parents. These factors are imprinted into the embryonic being at conception, as well as throughout the prenatal period - and can be identified as such, during conscious regressions.

A *third* strand of conception imprints are the actual *cellular memories* of the subjective experience of sperm and ovum, their origin (ovulation, spermatogenesis) and their climactic fusion encounter. These can also all be recollected in regressive memory journeys, often intertwined with awareness of the emotional state of one or both parents. The following two accounts illustrate how these kinds of connections may be made.

> (Male) – In one of the sessions, I actually felt being a sperm. It was quite an experience, all this force imprisoned in this little space waiting to burst out and convert the force into power. Since all I knew at that time was force, I was going to do this conversion with force. I felt being released from wherever I was and going down a tube with such fury, force and determination. I suddenly realized how throughout my life I have pushed and pushed for things I wanted done – with less than optimal results. My being born a premature baby is also consistent with this.

> (Female) – Slipping deeper in the prenatal phase, I sense myself as a tiny point, observing how the egg-cell of mother and seed-cell of father are approaching one another. I feel the reluctance of the egg-cell – she does not want to merge with the sperm-seed and become one. I feel this distinctly as my mother's resistance to merging with the male. She wants to stay within herself and feels the impending unity as threatening. I also feel my father's sperm-cell and the same resistance to merging with the ovum. Behind it is my father's suspiciousness towards the feminine. I distinctly recognize the resistance of both to the merging of sperm and ovum, and how this resistance to merging is built into every cell of my body. At first my reaction to this perception is dismay, shock, sadness and helplessness. But then there is also a calm acceptance of the reality of this original fertilization event.

Not only conception, but also discovery, implantation, placenta formation and other key events in embryogenesis, have recognizable, and potentially traumatic impacts in later character formation. At conception we are imprinted with the parents' attitudes towards love and sexuality – since conception occurs, after all, during a sexual experience of the parents. At *discovery*, when mother and father discover that conception has taken place (which may be up to two weeks after the conception event), we receive all their expectations, hopeful or fearful, of bearing a child, or another child, or a child of a particular gender.

In one workshop I took with William Emerson, he was asked what the effects were on later character formation if *conception and discovery were simultaneous*, i.e. *conscious and intentional*. Emerson replied that, on the basis of his observation of 20 to 30 such parent-child pairings, the children consciously conceived tended to have a particular kind of distinctive presence, almost a sense of entitlement, conveying their expectation that they would be respected and recognized for the spiritual being that they are. I immediately thought of my daughter, who was consciously conceived, and who quite clearly expresses this kind of attitude toward the world; whereas in myself, that kind of attitude has come only as a result of conscious work on myself as an adult.

At *implantation*, the embryo attaches into the uterine wall and develops a placenta and umbilical cord – through which it thereafter receives all of the mother's nutrients, energetic, biochemical and emotional. Since the navel/umbilicus junction is where these imprints come through during the prenatal period, contemplating this center with the purifying fires of enlightened awareness can serve to disentangle ancestral karmic imprints, as well maternal feelings about body, food and nurturing. Though the phrase "contemplating your navel" is a sarcastic put-down of narcissistic self-absorption, there may be some enlightenment value in the practice.

Whereas it is commonly believed that a life begins at conception, with the fertilization of an ovum, one could argue that, as with a plant or tree, the fertile seed has to be planted and rooted before it can start to grow. Embryologists estimate that as many as 50% of fertilized blastocytes don't make it through to implantation, i.e. are spontaneously eliminated or are re-absorbed into uterine tissue. Clearly, the mother's ability to nurture herself and to receive both physical and emotional nurturing is critical to a successful implantation.

The subjective experience of the implantation event, which may resonate throughout a person's life, even into adulthood, revolves around themes of security and groundedness – finding a place to live, a place in the world to put down roots, to feel safe and to be nourished. As Emerson writes, "every time we look for a home or even a place to stay for the night, we may be recapitulating our implantation journey." (Emerson, W., *Remembering Our Home*, p. 66)

One of the meditative divination processes I teach in my workshops is called *Unfolding the Tree of Your Life*. In it, we trace the analogical correspondences between the growth of a tree and the growth of a human life, and then create a tree drawing to portray our unique life course. In this process, birth corresponds to the moment when the rooted seedlings of the tree first push through the soil to the sunlight and the air above; the ancestral and genetic patterns correspond to the roots of the tree; and the seed planted in the dark earth corresponds to the fertilized ovum implanted in the nutrient–rich uterine wall, i.e. implantation

In North American Indian origin mythology, there are many variants of an *earth-diver myth,* symbolizing the sometimes hazardous implantation journey of the soul-cell. In such myths, a succession of different animals descend down into the primeval waters in order to secure a bit of sand or mud from which the earth is to be formed. One after another, the different animals fail, i.e. drown, until the last one succeeds in bringing up a small bit of mud between its claws or paws. Having brought this piece up to the surface of the waters, it then magically expands to become the earth as we know it and on which we live our lives. In just this way, once the fertilized egg-cell has found a place in the uterine wall where it can put down roots and be nourished – the process of first embryonic and then fetal growth can begin.

Soul memories from before conception

When prenatal regression therapists have pursued their inquiries to the time before conception, they have found memories of feelings and perceptions that seemingly come from a non-physical level of existence, yet with intimate awareness of the impending entry into the mother's womb. William Emerson identified two distinct feeling-complexes, coming from pre-conception, that can have long-lasting effects in a person's life, until resolved. One he called "divine homesickness," a feeling of wanting to return back to the heaven world from which one came; and the other "divine exile," a feeling of having been abandoned or exiled by God. Similarly, Ray Castellino has written that,

> "the way the primary consciousness leaves the other side sets up the primary existential dilemma of separation, aloneness, loss and longing in the individual. This is the dilemma of being on the earth, longing for the other side and being "a stranger in a strange land." (Castellino, R. *The Polarity Therapy Paradigm Regarding Pre-Conception.* p. 20)

Adults regressed to the pre-conception phase may recall a sense of floating in a non-physical space, near or around the mother and father, about to make a choice of some kind, a commitment to *come in* to a new life, or *come down* something like a tunnel or chute. They may recall having telepathic conversations with the mother and father, as well as with others who may be grandparents, or wise guides or angelic beings. Very young children will sometimes disclose these kinds of soul memories, if the parents are receptive. Even when reported by young children, the souls in such communications come across in a calm, re-assuring way.

> Mary, one of my students in the divination work, related that her four-year old daughter spontaneously told her mother that when she was "in heaven before," she kept urging her mother to "hurry up and get with Bill," the intended future husband and father, because she was eager to "get going and come in."

> A woman related that when she was a very young child of two or three, she told her mother that she remembered someone asking her to go and be born to her mother, because "she needed me." She remembered agreeing, and being in a blue light above where her mother was sleeping. "I somehow flashed inside of her." She remembered that her father didn't want her and gried to get the mother to abort the child – but she survived, as the mother stopped all drug use and turned her life around. (from Hallett, E. *Stories of the Unborn Soul*)

Miscarriages may be chosen by the unborn child, and announced in dreams to the parents. Communication may occur with a child-soul who has been conceived, but chooses not be born, out of compassion for the mother and father.

> The husband of a woman enduring a difficult pregacy with twins, dreamed of a young man coming to him and saying, "Dad, I have come to tell you that my sister and I have talked and we decided that now is not the time for both of us to come. She will come first, and I will come later when the time is right." It turned out that only one of the twins was viable. A healthy daughter was born and a brother followed twenty months later. (Hallett, E. *op.cit.*)

Whereas soul memories and communications seem to occur spontaneously in very young children, for adults they may occur in dreams or in deep hypnotic regressions, when we are somewhat freed from the usual time-space dimension. Or the communication may be mediated by a psychic.

> A couple had been trying to conceive a child, with one false start already. They were given a psychic reading by Alice Ann Parker, who was at that time channeling a Spirit Being named *Menos*. The couple had not talked to AAP about the conception project. In the middle of the session, AAP unexpectedly asked about a name, and said "it is someone important in your life, someone who inspires you." The next day they heard that the test had come back positive. Then they realized that the name must be the name of the child that had just arrived in her mother's womb and announced its arrival.

In my Alchemical Divination processes, after tuning in to the qualities absorbed from the parents at the time of conception, we will sometimes ask the question – *why did my soul choose this family to be born into?* In one such divination, a woman who was pregnant with her first child, found in herself a particularly strong connection to the mother line, and a sisterhood of mothers and daughters.

> I asked in the beginning why I chose my family because it seems to be an odd choice. When I was conceived, I realized that my mother recognized my father. My father didn't recognize my mother; but my mother recognized who my father was as a soul. It was like my soul was saying, "I need to remember to recognize you no matter what I go through in this life. When I see you, I'll recognize you."…I never had a sister, I only had a brother. I never knew what it's like to have sisters till now – I'm finding all my sisters, sisters that have been with me forever. That's why I'm here – to develop and strengthen that sisterhood. I felt the spiritual connection to the mother's lineage. And recognizing my mother and my grandmother as my sisters… and (my partner's daughters and his ex-wife as my sisters). I saw that I wasn't ready to be a mother until I had that experience, until I knew fully what it meant for a soul to make a choice to come into a body and fully what it means for her to come here and for me to recognize her. And Yeah, I'm having a girl.

Sometimes, the soul's choice of parents will seemingly reflect a working out of some karmic entanglement or indebtedness from another existence. Clients that I have guided in such soul journeys have sometimes said "choose my parents? Never in a thousand years would I choose those people," and I have to remind them we are speaking of soul, not personality. Paradoxically, a soul may choose a difficult family situation to be born into, for karmic reasons.

> A woman I worked with in such a soul journey found that her mission was to "learn to love," – a response that is often heard. It reflects the deep spiritual truth that the Earth path is a path of learning to serve and love others. I then questioned her further as to why her soul had chosen a family in which her mother regarded her with hatred and treated her with great cruelty. She replied that she had chosen to learn to love in a situation where love was hardly manifested to her as a child. We concluded that there must be a past-life karmic indebtedness between those two souls that they wanted or needed to work out. Further regression work would perhaps enable a disentanglement of those karmic threads.

The soul's choice of life path, family and associations, may relate to some lessons to be learned left over from another lifetime. As outsiders, we can never know the innermost details of another's soul-life or purpose. As parents, loved ones or friends of another, we can support each other in the unfolding of the soul's potential through unconditional love and understanding. Only the person themselves can access the core of their beingness where the essential soul vision is known and accepted.

> Peter, an only child who had a difficult relationship with his father, related that his father used to to say to him when he was younger, as a joke, "you know, I'm not your father, ha ha." This idiotic joke disturbed the son, who thought his father might abandon him. To me, the peculiar joke was a clue that perhaps there was a hidden karmic factor in the father-son relationship. Inquiring into Peter's father's history, it turned out that when he was a teenager, his father and his older brother had both died – leaving him without a male role model. During a regression trance, tuning in to the paternal lineage, I asked Peter whether *he* was perhaps the reincarnation of his father's

older brother, who had died young. His eyes tearing up seemed to confirm this soul connection, and it made sense of his father's cruel joke. For Peter's father, having no understanding of reincarnation, the memory of the past life relationship of the two brothers came through in this distorted way.

Family ancestral bonds may be interwoven with soul bonds. In dreams and visions, grandparents not uncommonly appear as guides or protectors for a child, or as messengers announcing a conception.

> From childhood on, a woman had repeated memories of sitting in her grandmother's lap. Her mother dismissed them as fantasies, since the grandmother had died six years before the girl was born. The memories persisted and the woman insisted she was with her grandmother "in a white room without walls." She said her grandmother was giving her guidance for her life to some. As she grew older she continued to dream about being the white room and receiving counsel from a source wise beyond her years (from Hallett, E. *op. cit.*).

Memories of soul connections between grandparents and grandchildren confirm the healing value that can reside in such relationships. In Jungian psychology, the relationship between *senex* and *puer* (or *senecta* and *puella*) is regarded as an archetypal image of an intrapsychic relationship – between the inner child and the wise elder within each of us. Nevertheless, under the best circumstances, the actual familial relationship bridging a generation, can be a most precious gift for both grandparent and grandchild. It makes sense – grandparents know the parents of the child from the other side, so to speak. They can offer balance and perspective otherwise easily lost in the emotional turbulence of our early years.

Connecting and reconciling with the ancestors

I have described what we have learned from hypnotic and divinatory regression practices about our prenatal existence and how one can come to experience remembering the presence of the soul around the time (or rather the event) of conception. From this work, I have come to understand that patterns in our psychic make-up that seemingly come from a time before conception, actually come from a timeless place in consciousness, beyond what we think of as the real world of time-and-space. I call this the place of *soul communion* where, in total agreement and unconditional love between the three souls of mother, father and child, the decision is made to incarnate in this particular family.

There is a deep knowing of the primary mission or purpose of one's life, one's chosen destiny and also an awareness and acceptance of karmic lessons to be learned or indebtedness to be paid. Intentionally connecting with the parents and then the parents of the parents, can be enormously healing and empowering to the individual and can lead to a greater knowing of one's purpose in life and a sense of having an unconditionally supportive back-up team. To develop a more meaningful connection with one's ancestors, it is useful to draw a chart of the major family relations known as a genogram.

Drawing an ancestral family genogram.

According to the convention developed by family systems therapists, the names of males are written in a square, females in a circle. You put yourself in the middle of the page, your mother's name in a circle above to the left, your father's in a square above to the right, with connecting lines between them and with your name. It's best to put their actual first name, not "Mom" or "Dad," to emphasize their autonomous personhood and soul. On the line next to your mother's and father's name, you can also list their sibings, your

> *aunts and uncles – particularly any that were in your life when you were growing up. On the line above the parents (i.e. "behind" if they were standing in front of you) put the squares and circles with the names of your four grandparents. You can include other ancestors further back than two generations, if you have reason to believe they are significant in your family history. You can list your sisters and brothers in the line next to your name; as well as your spouse or partner. And you can make a fourth line below yours with the children that you and your partner(s) have brought into the world. With each person's name you list the year of birth and death – if deceased. The purpose here is to have the basic facts of the family relationship lines in mind, when you make the ancestral connections.*

When beginning to tune in to the soul connection with their grandparents (or even parents, at times), some people will object that "I never knew them," or that they are long deceased. In our work with the alchemical divinations, both with and without entheogenic amplification, the vividness of the communication exchange with deceased ancestors that can occur, confirms the reality of a connection that transcends the boundaries of death and birth.

In this work, I have been deeply influenced by the family constellation approach of Bert Hellinger, who arranges a setting where individuals can have a dialogue or encounter with deceased ancestors through "representatives," who seem to embody these individuals in a mediumistic way. In the divination work that I have developed, you face the soul/spirits of the ancestors and elders on a kind of inner stage of consciousness and dialogue with them directly and respectfully. Although there are some exceptions, in our experience the ancestral spirits are usually delighted to be invited to connect – as most grandparents would be to connect with their grandchildren while still alive.

Just experiencing the presence of an unconditional support of the ancestors (beyond the parents) can be hugely empowering and liberating, *especially* in situations where the person may never have outwardly "known" the grand-parents while alive. People are often astounded and delighted to feel, for the first time, the continuity and strength of their two lineages, and to know the connection with ancestral souls that are no longer alive – but still related. It helps put the personality conflicts and differences of the current life into deeper perspective.

> (Female) It was really amazing to connect with my family. I've spent so much time looking at, and working with, the wounding of my family and it was just awesome to hold them like this and just fully embrace all of them. I could just see a picture of all of them in front of me in…the barrenness of Eastern Oregon where we lived, where I was a child, and the hard work clothing that they wore. Just wrapping myself around who they were, there was so much joy that came from that and I could feel that joy and the laughter. They're tough as nails, they are strong people and really full of so much courage. They were farmers, immigrants from Sweden. I felt them right at my back. I've never let myself really bring them in that closely because of the abuse in the family and so it was really just quite a comfort and also can see how much their adventurous and pioneering spirit is how I am.

> (Male) I had never met my maternal grandmother, but in my vision she was delighted that I would approach and was beaming. I was really surprised, beause she, in the family mythology, was always sort of discounted. So I was happy to have that radiance and that sense that I was a part of her. An uncle, her son, died suddenly from a heart attack and I had some strife with him. He and I really connected. He was just kind of gruff and I was unskilled in our interactions and I just said to him, 'Hey man', and he said, 'Hey man. It's okay', and it was just a wonderful kind of heart connection. And all the stuff was just obviously such crap, such hubris. And I said, 'I just really want you on my team'. And he said, 'I am on your team'. Dead about 12 years now, I think. So that was really wonderful.

> (Female) The piece when the ancestors came to me - it was both lineages at the same time. I walked into a room and both sides were there. My father's lineage was a Jewish trip and little people in black and white huddling and

praying. And my mother's side they were holding together for dear life, clenching onto each other with lots of food. My father's family was hanging on to education and diplomas for dear life. Everybody was hanging on for dear life. They came and they said to me "You've known this all along. Your job is to change this. Your job is to shift out of this Jewish fear…and we are all here to support you to do it." Then…I felt like I'm rooted in my new paradigm to start the journey. And so my journey was just total joy. And the ease of being in the body…the whole thing was so embodied, so connected to the spirit and so belonging - three things I have not felt in my fifty years: ease in the body, joy and belonging.

Connecting with the ancestral lineage is not necessarily always experienced as unconditionally supportive – at least at first. In many indigenous societies with living shamanic traditions in Africa and Asia, family or individual afflictions are often seen to have originated in some action offensive to the ancestors – and then require some kind of propitiating ritual to heal. In the examples below, the connection with the ancestors resulted in some kind of confrontation, requiring recognition and reconciliation before the familial support would be granted.

The following experience was reported by a participant in one of my groups – an American Jewish man married to a non-Jewish German woman.

> As I asked to connect with my ancestors I became aware of rows and rows of my Jewish ancestors, several of them Rabbis, dating back to Middle Ages. I was surprised to notice however, as I greeted them, that they did not seem to be particularly friendly towards me or welcoming. The attitude they conveyed was cold and distanced. When I asked, telepathically, as to the reason for their withholding of support – it was made clear to me that they questioned my choice of a German woman for my mate. I then explained to them the history of my relationship with her, what my wife meant to me and the qualities that led me to choose her – over the traditionally expected choice of a Jewish girl. The ancestors listened to my account and then nodded to indicate their satisfaction with my explanation. The encounter ended with a celebratory honoring of our connection and our lineage.

In the following account, a man in Germany describes how he was able to heal a deep sense of shame that afflicted the males in his family for generations.

I laid both hands over my eyes, which induces darkness and countless peaceful star-like patterns of light – and brings me to the council of ancestral souls. There I ask – why is the father lineage black and as if cut-off? I had asked before about this but didn't get an answer. Now I see the men are weak, drunkards, liars. (In my family) one didn't speak of them. I was never proud of my paternal name, nor of the place in which I was born. I left home at the age of 18 with repugnance. Then I ask my council of ancestral souls what it was that oppressed the men – besides the poverty and the wars and probably also the crimes in which they surely participated. I see a female figure – it must be my great-grandmother, about whom I know nothing. I'm receiving thoughts and images and recognize – she sold herself in the saloon. I see her in a side room, lifting her long, black skirt. She had to do it in order to feed her family – the men couldn't do it on their own. That was the family shame – the men couldn't make it by themselves.

And I'm seeing a further aspect of this situation – that the prostitution of the clanmother was known in the village, and was mocked by the men in the saloons and in the coal-mine, the big employer in the area. This great-grandmother wanted to liberate at least one of her sons out of poverty and send him to America to freedom and paradise. And she did succeed in taking care of her children – that shame was the price that she and the men in the family paid. I was doubtful of this vision and asked for confirmation – and the images became even clearer and more detailed. I realize that in the figure of this great-grandmother lies the key to my resistance to my paternal lineage. Then I'm speaking with one of her grandsons, my uncle Hans, who spent the last years of his life in bed, living on beer. Why couldn't his two brothers pull him out of his alcoholic swamp – always this impotence among the men. I also talk with my uncle Fritz and my grandfather – and forgive them, letting it be. And then I'm filled with deep joy and strength and can stand up say "I am of this family, from this place." I feel complete and rooted on two legs.

In the following account of a visionary divination, a psychically-gifted woman of mixed African-American, Native American and white Euro-American ancestry, who had done extensive genealogical research on her lineages, describes how she came to some surprising and heart-opening realizations through direct spiritual encounters with her racially entangled ancestors. Her first symbolic visions were of the Green Tara and the goddess Sophia.

Sophia faded into a circle of brilliant white light, and my maternal great grandfather, BW, who died before I was born, appeared out of an unfolding white light. He was wearing brown work clothes. Instinctively I knew who he was. BW was brought to America on a slave ship. His son, my grandfather S, was the first generation removed from slavery. He also died before I was born and my grandmother was forever telling me how smart he was and how much she loved him.

In this vision, BW appeared as a medium built African man about forty years old with a large white Afro, a heavy white mustache and smooth black skin. The stern facial expression and fixed stare with which he gazed on me addressed a prejudice I have a spent a lifetime concealing. Uneasiness and guilt tugged at me. I was dumbfounded and didn't know what to say. He extended his right hand off to the side. I turned to see what he was offering. There in an open field before me were six young black men hanging by the neck, from a tree. Every part of me knew I was related to those young men. A deep sense of remorse came over me. I felt ashamed. All the years of denying and rejecting the African side of the family and their contribution to my being, had not gone un-noticed by those who paved the way for my being. They are those upon whose shoulders I stand. Grandpa B was there to hold me to task. He knew I was listening because he held out his left hand, and let his right hand fall to his side. The men hanging faded. I turned my attention to B's left and the march of my paternal grandmothers started to unfold.

The first image was that of a compassionate round-faced African woman in her early forties. Her thick silver and black streaked hair had been pressed to shoulder lnegth. The black housedress she wore suited her medium sized body. Her steps were light as she moved towards me in full body. She then stepped off to the side and faded from view, as did those who followed behind her. The era out of which the grandmothers emerged was reflected in their hairstyles and their dress. When the march began to wind down from what seemed like hours, Indian and white grandmothers showed themselves.

After their appearance and disappearance, a cloud with an Indian chief wearing a large head dress of large white feathers embedded in a red and brown headband with small feathers, wearing a soft animal skin blanket unfolded. This maternal ancestor was sitting on the ground with his legs folded, drawing a circle in the dirt with a green twig. He looked like a white man. For the most part he looked at the ground. When he did look up, however, he looked at me with a stern look, like the one BW had presented. I knew the chief to be my maternal ancestor S. who lived seven generations ago. I had written S.'s family history, honoring his life work. S was born in 1781, the third son of an English settler and an Indian woman. He founded a town for free people of color and when he died was recognized as one of the wealthiest men in Tennessee. His family was multicultural. They say Indians believe that each person is responsible for seven generations. I am the great granddaughter of his eldest grandson, a member of the seventh generation. Grandma Betty was the fifth generation. Her father was German, and her mother Cherokee. It wasn't until Grandma Betty married an African, the youngest son of BW, that a family member moved away from their European/Native American mix.

S had twenty-five slaves and when slavery ended there was a battle to keep family members from marrying freed slaves. Thus the race war began and was carried on by my grandmother. She was forever telling us not to fraternize or marry a dark-skinned man, forgetting that she was the first to introduce Africans into the bloodline. I tried to figure out what S was angry about as I sat there watching him. I didn't know if he was angry about the way I had recorded the history (of the family). I was feeling overwhelmed by it all when BW reappeared and surprised me by sitting down next to S. I looked at them sitting there together, talking and smiling, and realized there was solidarity in the mix. As soon as that realization came, BW smiled at me. The men were seated in a circle talking. I couldn't hear what they were saying but I felt comfortable watching them. I noticed that there weren't any women present, and the guide suggested that I ask the men to invite the women. I framed the request in thought, which over the years, I have learned to do when communicating with the spirits.

Suddenly, a line of tall beautiful Black women, who I knew to be Watusies, entered dancing. They were naked from the waist up, wearing beautiful jeweled neck-to-waist dickies, with matching headbands. Their torsos were covered with large white feather skirts that hugged their waist loosely. On their right leg they wore rainbow colored ankle bracelets. The rhythm and the noise they made when they danced brought a smile to my face, made me happy. A smiling S appeared, followed by the Goddess Sophia, who slowly faded into the Christ body as he emerged from her, sitting amidst a garden of flowers and lotus petas. The sun came out. I felt the tribal wars were over, and that I was forgiven.

I felt that I had accomplished what I had set out out to do, at least in the short term. I realized the openings by no means completed the task or did the work that these types of openings require. Decayed roots were exposed; the practice of recognizing and attending them when they appear in my daily life was the work. And for that learning I am grateful to grandfathers and grandmothers.

Recognizing one's life path and purpose

In the ancestral divination rituals, after connecting with family, ancestors and guides to resolve outstanding questions or difficulties, I will also usually suggest that people ask about their life-path, their work and purpose. Not surprisingly perhaps, one's chosen life-work is not infrequently connected to the family history, directly or indirectly. In my own case, I shared a love of books with my father, who was a bibliophile and publisher, like his father. But when he invited me to join in the family book publishing business, I declined by saying that I was more interested in the writing of books than in the producing and publishing end (although now I'm involved with that as well).

> (Female) When I went into my ancestral lineage I realized in regard to my grandfathers and my father, the males in my family – I had not been so attuned to them. On my mother's side my grandfather was an aviation engineer. My mother's grandfather was a painter, who painted all these paintings of the Missions and the Indians. And then on my dad's side, my dad's father was a musician and was also a very successful business man. So I spent a lot of time asking my father's father about how to become a musician. And he gave me some very practical information, you know, to practice and the next place to have a room big enough for the piano. So that was wonderful.

> (Male) I came into the council of ancestral souls and experienced clearly and distinctly their great benevolence toward my chosen life-work, especially from my father and paternal grandfather. They were smiling at me, encouraging me in my vision, and simultaneously communicating their wish that I won't disconnect from them, because they themselves in their lives did not succeed in completely manifesting their vision. I understood directly that my father's soul vision was similar to mine, and recognized that I have, up until now, cut myself off from the power of his potential support. I saw that I had done this because I was blinded by his failure to manifest his vision – which I also saw was the reason for his relatively early death (at 57). Great respect for my father and grandfather arose in me, and as I bowed to them inwardly, I received the guidance to be more resolute in expressing my vision of being a model for others, in my work as trainer and coach. Our world needs models, they said – especially now. They added that, after all, I had inherited my drive and energy from them – which is true! As I left the meeting with the council of ancestral souls I felt, for the first time, their

strength supporting my back – which is wonderfully empowering. This feeling lasted – in the following days I felt fortunate to have met the souls of my ancestors and to feel their blessing for me and my life vision.

The ancestral soul communion can yield surprising insights into one's interests, when these had been assumed to be quite separate from the family – as in the following account from a woman artist deeply interested in shamanism.

> I realized that both my parents are very expressive with their hands in the arts. They were always making things. My father's a wood worker, an incredible artist. My mother too, was always making things. She was always creating things and giving them away. She was an herbalist. And her family were like closet poets. I saw this whole lineage of bards and poets and singers way back there. And I already knew about this but I hadn't connected it, that there was all this shamanic energy in that lineage and somewhere in the last three hundred years it just got totally buried.

Sometimes in such guided regression divinations, in addition to the council of deceased parents and ancestors, one can become aware of the presence of a council of elders, somehow behind and higher than the ancestors (although sometimes they are mingled). These are recognized as beings with whom we have a guiding and teaching relationship that may persist over many lifetimes. In Chapter Four, I will discuss experiences with this higher council, who function as spiritual guides for the immortal soul in working out its karmic lessons and evolutionary challenges.

Three

Death and Hereafter

A cartoon published in the newsletter of the *Association for Pre- and Perinatal Psychology* shows twin fetuses side by side in their womb vessel prior to birth. One of them asks: "Is there life after birth?" The other one replies "We don't know. No one has come back to tell us." The joke points to the paradoxical analogy between the experience of birth and death – an analogy that has become even more apparent through the research in pre- and perinatal psychology described in the previous chapter. This work has revealed that a human birth is not only a process of mammalian physiology but the subjective experience of a soul emerging into a radically new and unknown phase of its earthly existence.

Birth and death have always been the accepted and conventional boundary transitions framing a human life. The personal story of our existence in human society is told and remembered as lasting between the date of birth and date of death. What comes after death – "the undiscovered country, from whose bourn no traveler returns" – has remained the great mystery, shadowed by feelings of fear and loss and grief. In this chapter we will discuss the findings of researchers in thanatology and near-death experience (NDE), as well as certain philosophical and spiritual teachings, that shed new light on death and dying. We can see that, here too, the physiological processes of bodily death are accompanied by the subjective experience of a soul going through a great phase transition from the known to the terrifyingly unknown.

Not only are birthing and dying phenomenologically similar transitions, they are intimately intermingled in both physiology and experience. As Stanislav Grof has written, "birth is a potential or actual life-threatening event. The delivery brutally terminates the intrauterine existence of the fetus. He or she "dies" as an aquatic organism and is born as an air-breathing, physiologically and even anatomically different form of life." (*The Psychology of the Future*, 2000, p. 32).

Buddhist, Hindu and other esoteric teachings of reincarnation and rebirth speak of a three-fold sequence – death, an intermediate phase or afterlife, and then rebirth. Elaborate cartographies exist in many cultures, so-called *Books of the Dead*, describing the landscape of the afterlife. We can recognize here a convergence of the experience of birthing and dying: the passage through the birth canal is *at once the death of the fetal self and the birth of a newborn human self.* If the process of birthing is inevitably accompanied (or preceded) by a kind of dying, is it then also true that the process of dying is accompanied (or followed) by a kind of birth into a new and vastly expanded world?

Just such an idea can be found in the writings of the remarkable 19th century German scientist, scholar and philosopher Gustav Theodore Fechner (1801-1887). Fechner is regarded in the history of psychology as one of the founders of experimental psychology. He was trained as physicist, and taught and wrote on science, but had a mystical bent and a phenomenally broad range of interests. Fechner damaged his eye-sight in experiments that involved looking at the sun, and had to spend almost a year in complete darkness. When he emerged from this accidental death-rebirth initiation, he was clairvoyant and wrote books on *The Soul Life of Plants* and *The Comparative Anatomy of Angels*.

In 1835, in response to a friend's loss of a loved one, he wrote a short book called *Das Büchlein vom Leben nach dem Tode* (The Little Book of Life After Death). William James, who greatly admired Fechner, wrote an introduction to the English translation, which appeared in 1904. The book is remarkable, as much for its tone, which is visionary, almost oracular, as for the content, which is completely free of any religious terminology, yet formulates a sophisticated psycho-philosophical position about the reality of the after-life and consciousness after death. The first of the nine brief chapters deals with the phenomenological parallels between death and birth. The following is my translation of the opening passage.

> Man lives upon the Earth not once, but three times. The first phase is a continuous sleep, the second an alternation between sleeping and waking, and the third phase a continuous waking. In the first phase we live alone, in darkness; in the second, we live among others but separate, and in a light which reflects the outer surface of things; in the third phase our life is intertwined with that of other spirits, in the higher life of the Great Spirit, and we see into the ultimate reality of things.
>
> In the first phase the body develops from the seed-cell, and creates the equipment needed for the second phase; in the second phase the soul develops from its seed-origin and creates the tools for the third phase. In the third phase, the seed of the divine which lies in every human soul, develops in what is for us a darkness – though we may know of what lies beyond the human through intuition, belief, feeling, or the instincts of genius; but for the Spirit in the third phase it is as bright as daylight.
>
> The transition from the first to the second phase we call birth; the transition from the second to the third phase we call death. The pathway from the second to the third phase is no more dark and obscure than the pathway from the first to the second. The one leads to outer perception of the world, the other to interior vision.

Just as the fetus (child) in the first phase is still blind and deaf to all the radiance and the music of life in the second phase; and as the birth from the warm body of the mother is hard and painful; and as there comes a time during the birthing when the destruction of its prior existence must feel like a dying, before the awakening to the new exterior way of being, -- so do we, in our present existence, in which our entire consciousness is still bound with the confining body, perceive nothing of the radiance and the music, the splendor and the freedom, of life in the third phase; and readily think of the dark and narrow passage which takes us there as a blind alley with no exit. But our death is only a second birth into a freer beingness, in which the soul breaks through and leaves behind its narrow sheath, just as the child did at the time of its birth.

The experience of dying

Modern accounts of near-death experiences (NDEs), in which someone dies in an accident or during surgery and then returns, have identified many of the same features found in traditional and mythic descriptions of this ultimate transition. They say there is a sense of sudden discontinuity, a lifting-off into an out-of-body (OBE) state and entering into an upward sloping tunnel of increasing brightness. This may then be followed by meeting with previously deceased parents or ancestors, accompanied by a sense of welcoming and homecoming. Some of the NDE accounts tell of meeting a spirit guide or angelic being and receiving divine wisdom and guidance for their return to physical life.

Of course, we have no way of knowing to what extent these very positive features reported in NDE accounts are also found in ordinary deaths that are not followed by a return to earthly existence. As with the subjective experience of being born, we can imagine an enormous variability, depending on the level of spiritual development and preparation of the individual soul. Some who die suddenly and unexpectedly, and without a worldview that accommodates any notion of an after-life, may indeed find themselves hovering around their empty physical vehicle, a restless ghost in a disoriented *limbo* state, "neither here nor there."

Traditional and contemporary descriptions converge for the situation when the dying occurs gradually and as expected, in the course of illness or old age. At the moment of expiration, the taking and releasing of the last few breaths, there occurs what is called a "separation of the elements." No longer held together by circulating spiritual life-force, the earth and water elements naturally sink downward, as the prone body becomes cold and clammy from the feet up. The *Tibetan Book of the Dead* calls this symptom "earth sinking into water" and Taoist texts speak of the fluid *ching* energy of the pelvic cauldron naturally flowing downward and outward, when no longer circulated upward by the life-force.

Air and fire elements naturally rise upward – as the electric *chi* energy radiating from the solar plexus center becomes faint, sensations of clammy coldness may be accompanied by feverish heat. According to the Taoists, the volatile *shen* energy of the throat and head disperses naturally upward, but during life is drawn down and circulated through the body with the breath. When the last breath of air is drawn and released, the *shen* escapes – we say the person has "expired" or "given up the ghost."

There is, in the process of dying, a kind of physiological unwinding, a slowing down and progressive shutting off of vital functions, which may or may not be accompanied by cellular pathology and degeneration. The process at some point probably involves the release of endorphins, the body's own pain-reducing chemicals, which may account for the often calm and peaceful demeanor of one who is on the final threshold. The subjective similarity of dying with going to sleep, our nightly instinctive release from the physical realm, is reflected in the Greek myth of *Thanatos* and *Hypnos* as twin brother deities – both robed and winged escorts for the out-of-body journey to the other side. Perhaps the sweetest exemplar of peaceful dying is to make the final transition while the body rests in sleep.

A sense of crossing a threshold and of departing on a long journey into an unknown future commonly accompanies the process, often with a mixture of excitement and anxiety. The journey of dying contains a paradox: we know for certain we are leaving, on a journey with no returning, but we don't know where we're going or what we will experience. This paradoxical indefiniteness is expressed in phrases such as "passing on," "leaving form," or passing to the "other side." This acute and terrifying paradox probably accounts for the continuing fascination with the reports of NDEs – reports from travelers who *have* returned – that regularly land on best-seller lists.

My personal favorite of the metaphors for what comes after death, is the *hereafter*. In once mentioned to Ram Dass that I thought his famous epigram *Be Here Now* could be extended, so to speak, by adding to it —*and Hereafter*. It would apply the practice of being-here-now to our after-death state. He chuckled appreciatively at the phrase – and then said that *Be Here Now* was sufficient, since it covered both realms. Being consciously in the here-now when in the after-death realms, is in fact the essence of the Tibetan Buddhist *bardo* teachings.

Timothy Leary, in a filmed conversation with Ram Dass shortly before his death, expressed a sense of adventure and calm acceptance at the journey to come. He had arrived at this attitude after relinquishing his earlier project to freeze his brain through cryogenics for some potential future technological resuscitation.

Before the modern era of heroic life-extending medical interventions, such an accepting attitude was perhaps more common in earlier generations. A woman in one of my workshops in Sweden related how her grandfather seemed to know when his time was coming. One evening he assembled his family, said a last goodnight and good-bye to everyone, and laid down to sleep on his bed, keeping his clothes and shoes on. He wanted to be appropriately dressed for the long journey to come, as he said.

> **Divination to Your Dying Day**
>
> *To prepare yourself, find a quiet time and place in your life and enter into a meditative space. Center awareness and identity in the Cave of the Heart, which is the whole chest cavity from the shoulders to the upper abdomen. Invoke the blessings and assistance of your teacher(s) and/or Spirit Guide(s). Ignite the purifying light-fire energy-sun in the Heart-Center and concentrate on the presence of empathy and equanimity. Envision yourself walking on the road of your life, remembering the scenes of your youth and middle years, and coming, probably at some point in your elder years, to the place where you realize, and accept without denial or reservation, but with equanimity and compassion, that this life of yours will end.*
>
> *Some people may choose to ask at what age they will die and what will be the physical cause of their demise. I only suggest you tune into your state of mind and body when you come to realize you are in the last year of your life. What is it like for you then? Where are you living? Who are you living with – your partner, your children, your grandchildren? How are you with your family? Then refocus the telescope of time and tune into your state of mind and body in*

> *the last month of your life, when you will have disengaged more completely from all your earthly commitments and engagements. What is it like for you then – how would you like it to be – who would you like to be there with you? Will you ask to have a spiritual counselor or advisor? Will you be saying good-byes to close relatives and friends? And your last day – how will that be for you – as you embark on the great adventure?*

The image of dying as an adventurous journey may be conveyed to the living through dream-state communication from the departed. After my father Wolfgang had died, I dreamed that I met him on a mountain hiking trip in the Alps. He had often taken me and my brothers on such trips when we were young, and I cherished happy memories of these adventures. In the dream, I was with a group of friends in Switzerland (which corresponded to my waking life experience at the time) and we met Wolfgang in a small Alpine village with cobble-stone streets. He looked hale and hearty, though he was carrying a heavy backpack, as was his custom when we had gone hiking. My friends and I talked with him for while, delighted at the meeting. Then he said good-bye and walked slowly upward, on the cobble-stone street of the village and beyond into the mountains. I watched him for a while as he climbed – and then I returned with my friends down into the valley.

A different, even opposite metaphor for the experience of dying is also found in many mediumistic and mythic accounts: that of taking off clothes or masks, of releasing or dropping our familiar form to enter into a completely new kind of existence. The contemporary medium channeling a spirit-being called *Bartholomew*, suggested that we think of the process rather like taking off an old pair of shoes, that have become ill-fitting and uncomfortable.

The metaphor of the removing of outer coverings or layers is also found in the epitaph that Benjamin Franklin, who was by trade a printer, wrote for himself. He imagined his body "like the cover of an old book, it's contents torn out, stripped of its lettering and gilding, lies here, food for worms." Franklin wrote further, attesting to his belief in reincarnation, that "the work shall not be lost, for it will, as he believed, appear once more, in a new and more elegant edition, revised and corrected – by the Author."

The tradition of the three-day transition

Many indigenous and traditional cultures preserve the belief that in ordinary deaths the soul's transition to the liberated state of the after-death world involves a three-day period of struggle and confusion. This is the basis for the custom, for example among the Irish, of a three-day "wake" in which the surviving relatives are requested to remain awake and conscious, perhaps to sing and to lament, but also to tell stories of the deceased and celebrate his or her life. The wakeful conscious state of the surviving relatives assists the departing traveler, to whom they are related by the bonds of family and friendship, as he or she negotiates the turbulent and frightening passage to the world beyond.

My teacher Russell Schofield explained that the reason for the traditional three-day wake has to do with the *etheric matrix* or *double*. This is the subtle body that is an exact duplicate form at the physical time-space dimension, but with slightly higher vibratory frequency, and hence normally invisible. This means it can pass through solid walls and it can fly. It accompanies us throughout life, maintains the integrity of the physical form in sickness and health, and leaves the physical vehicle nightly parked in sleep. Though we may remember our soul journeys in other worlds and dimensions in the rich symbolic imagery of our dreams, the journeys of the etheric double in the ordinary time-space dimension of our world occur mostly unconsciously – except in lucid dreams of flying or in the out-of-body travels of advanced yogic practitioners, clairvoyant seers and remote-viewers.

As my teacher explained, although the etheric double can disengage easily enough for the nightly out-of-body journeys of sleep and dreams, the more complete disengagement called for at the time of the death of the physical vehicle takes longer. Particularly the disentanglement from the brain, because of the multi-layered complexity of neural circuits and conditioned thought-feeling memory patterns, ordinarily takes about three days – and is likely to be experienced as subjectively confusing and frightening. We can see how the mindful and even celebratory wakefulness of loving companions would be a valuable source of light and comfort during this complex maneuver. Of course, the difficulties are likely to be compounded if the death occurs suddenly and unexpectedly. Yet, as traditional spiritual teachings have averred, ministering helpers from the other side and angelic guides are always present to help ease the pain of a difficult and unexpected transition.

Even such a very high-level adept as the Master Jesus of Nazareth was apparently subject to (or more likely, chose to undergo) the three-day period of disentangling from the low-frequency conditioned earth-elements of the physical body. This is probably the meaning of the phrase in the Apostolic Creed

– *descendit ad infernos* ("he descended to the lower regions"), and after three days and nights returned to Earth, met with some of the disciples and then ascended to the higher celestial realms. Although this Biblical story has caused theological discomfort among certain Christian denominations, who can't fathom how or why Jesus would descend to "hell," as it is usually, and erroneously, translated. But it makes perfect sense when we think of it as his intentional and conscious exemplary modeling of the usual human experience of bodily death and purification.

The *underworld* of classical mythology, like the *lower world* of worldwide shamanic traditions, is not at all like the hell of the early Christian writers – a place of unending pain and punishment. The lower world/underworld is the place souls go to first, right at or after the death of the physical body, when the subjective experience is often dominated by anguish, grief, denial and negativity. The soul is disentangling itself from the densest, heaviest parts of the mortal vehicle, loaded with the residues of illusory and distorted self-images acquired in the human life that just ended. The Master Jesus, as a highly advanced adept, did not need to pass through the infernal region when his body died – but apparently used the occasion to visit this world and give aid and comfort to the disoriented and troubled souls hovering there.

Near-Death, Ego-Death and Transcendence

In my book *MindSpace and TimeStream* I discussed how a near-death experience (NDE) could be understood in terms of an altered state of consciousness in which the catalyst or trigger is the perception that the vital functions of the physical body, particularly the heart, have actually stopped. The clock-time of the typical NDE (established after the fact) can vary from a few minutes to a half-hour or more. Subjectively, the time-space dimension is completely transcended, as the experiences remembered and reported seem to occur in a timeless and dimensionless realm. The sense of being in a different time stream is one of the strongest indications of a profoundly altered state of consciousness.

Although the dilation and transcendence of time and space is also characteristic of high intensity psychedelic experiences, in other respects the so-called "ego-death" experiences of drug-induced or holotropic states is quite different. In such states, a person may subjectively *feel as if* they are dying, indeed struggle for a long period of time resisting dying, when there is actually no objective indication of physiological death or even nearness to death. My good friend and mentor, the late Leo Zeff, told me of an experience he had with ayahuasca in which he felt he was being devoured by a giant serpent, struggling, heaving and twisting for six hours – until he finally gave up resisting, let himself be devoured – and was instantly released into an ecstatic, liberated state.

Over the past forty years, I have collected, compiled and published four collections of accounts of psychedelic experiences – with LSD, MDMA, ayahuasca and psilocybe mushrooms – which cover a wide range of ecstatic, heavenly as well as agonizing, hellish experiences. However, psychedelic experiences rarely, if ever, involve the features of classic near-death experience – such as looking down on one's dead body from above (OBE) or meeting deceased relatives and angelic escorts. I suspect that the crucial distinguishing feature that occurs in NDEs and not in psychedelic "ego-death" experiences is the perception, at some level, that the heart has actually stopped.

In addition to complete transcendence of time and space, positive psychedelic experiences typically involve feelings of ecstatic liberation or blissful dissolution of illusory boundaries between self and other, or between self and world. There may be fleeting thoughts or perceptions of bodily death in such an experience, or none at all. Indeed, all the usual conceptions of physical form or existence may be transcended and considered completely irrelevant.

As an example, here is an excerpt of my description of an experience I had from smoking the vaporized exudate of the venom of the Colorado River toad *(bufo alvarius),* which contains *5-methoxy-DMT* (a substance also found naturally in the human pineal gland, and in certain shamanic plants).

> A shattering annihilation, a feeling of being inside a nuclear explosion, being fragmented into countless tiny shards. I felt as though I was being turned inside out, like my innards were extruding through my mouth. My body was rolling on the ground, coiled into a ball, like the ourobouros serpent. I opened my eyes momentarily and could see that I was protected by my friends from bumping into things or rolling into the fireplace. Instant reality check. Eyes closed, I was immersed again into the swirling, seething synaesthetic maelstrom, in which all distinctions between inner and outer, self and other, even directions like above and below, were obliterated. Animal sounds appeared to be coming from my mouth. There were no feelings of fear, indeed no feelings at all, other than a kind of impersonal ecstasy. No sense of body, no sense of self, no "I".
>
> Images of decapitation, dismemberment, disembowelment flashed by, in rapid succession, including an image of being run through the chest with a sword, -- yet there was no fear or horror associated with these images. The following thoughts occurred: "Death comes to all, now it's your turn, this is it, the termination. Resistance is impossible and pointless. Besides, it's too late, annihilation has already happened."
>
> When I let go within, there were feelings of great peacefulness and a soft breathing in the heart. I gently approached knots of contraction or pain. Out of a hard nugget of pain, in the groin, a serenely exploding flare of light energy spread throughout the body. The softly ascending light flare sparkled with jewels and precious stones, as if the pain had been a locked-up

treasure chest. Multi-colored lines of light formed a kind of dome covered in a faceted geometric network of jewels, the whole dome spinning silently clockwise. The jeweled dome seemed to become a kind of lens through which I could see into other worlds beyond, where the points of light were stars and galaxies.

As I gradually came back into my body, after ten minutes in real time, I felt bathed in pure joy and completely at peace with myself, the world and my death (Metzner, R. *Homage to the Visionary Toad*, 2003).

On the other hand, negative, hellish or "bad trip" psychedelic experiences may indeed involve the person's *fear that he/she is dying or has died,* accompanied by the delusion that perhaps one has taken a toxic overdose, as well as the belief that one has now done irreparable brain damage or gone permanently insane. Such fears may exist in spite of it being abundantly evident to others that all physiological signs in the individual are entirely normal. In such terrifying bad trip situations, as well as in dealing with the anxiety that naturally accompanies the amplified transcendence of our normal conceptions of reality, it is clear that the wise counsel recorded in one or another of the world's spiritual traditions on preparing for death could be supremely valuable.

When the individual recovers or returns from such a painful ego-death experience, there may indeed also be a sense of being reborn – into a new and larger life-world. The literature of psychedelic experiences is filled with such dramatic death-rebirth epiphanies. Just as actual birth is an expansion of awareness following the death of the fetal ego, so does spiritual rebirth and renewal follow the death or transcendence of the old ego-self.

New and ancient ways of preparing for dying

In our 1964 book *The Psychedelic Experience,* Leary, Alpert and I, following a suggestion from Aldous Huxley, had adapted the *Tibetan Book of the Dead* as a paradigm for a spiritually-oriented psychedelic experience. With appropriate preparation and orientation, so we proposed, psychedelic travelers could be guided, or guide themselves, to release their ego-attachments and illusory self-images, the way a Tibetan Buddhist *lama* would guide a dying man or woman to relinquish their attachments while noting the physical signs of the death of the body. In the years since that publication, I (and my co-authors) have received numerous letters expressing the grateful appreciation of readers who used it to prepare themselves for spiritually transcendent psychedelic experiences.

In the course of experiencing and confronting the fears of transcending the physical body, they could recognize they were significantly reducing their fears of dying and coming to a peaceful acceptance of their mortality. Indeed, experiencing the transcendence of your physical identification, with the certain knowledge that your essence, your spiritual core, your soul, persists beyond the boundary of bodily death is without doubt the most precious gift that psychedelic experiences can provide.

This was the gift vouchsafed in the mystery religions of ancient civilizations, where initiates went through an experience of death and rebirth, in which they were provided a vision of the reality of the spiritual worlds beyond. We do not know the details of what was involved in these religions, since initiates were sworn to secrecy. However, in the case of the Eleusinian Mysteries, which was for two thousand years the fountain-head of Western spirituality, the scholarly and pharmacological researches related by R. Gordon Wasson, Albert Hofmann, and Carl Ruck in their book *The Road to Eleusis,* have demonstrated with high probability that the ingestion of an LSD-like ergot derivative was involved.

The relevance of spiritually-oriented and guided psychedelic experiences in alleviating death anxiety and helping prepare people for the ultimate transition has found modern expression and application in medical-psychiatric research. Stanislav Grof and Joan Halifax, in their book *The Human Encounter with Death* described the work they did using the tryptamine DPT, with patients suffering from terminal cancer. More recently, psychiatrist Charles Grob, working at UCLA, has done studies using psilocybin (the active ingredient in the visionary mushroom of ancient Mexico) with people with a diagnosis of terminal cancer. It is a significant expansion of the accepted medico-scientific worldview that a medicine can be approved that has not been shown to effect a cure of an illness – but rather to alleviate the normal, human end-of-life anxiety.

> A woman with end-stage cancer who participated in this study, related (in a filmed interview) how all her fears about death, her guilt and worries about surviving family members, congealed into a kind of mass that pressed on her chest, squeezing her life-force – and then, as the psilocybin medicine came on, simply dissolved. At that exact moment she had the insight that all her fears and worries were about a future that had not yet happened. She realized that she could choose instead to focus her attention on the life she still had, with its love of family, the beauty and pleasure afforded by her garden and even a renewed devotion to improving her well-being through yoga.

Studies such as this have led visionary physicians and scientists of consciousness to consider the far-reaching possibilities of future care for the dying, involving selective use of entheogenic medicines. While the growth of the hospice movement, involving palliative in-home pain-management, is an encouraging sign, the mainstream medical establishment still tends to regard death as an outcome to be aggressively delayed and prevented. With an expanded spiritual worldview that recognizes the continuity of life after death and the possibilities of communication with the spirits of the dead, one can envision centers, in beautiful natural environments, in which meditative practices with guided psychedelic amplification could be offered for those in the final stage of life.

Just such centers for preparation for the dying were envisioned by Aldous Huxley (1894-1963), in his last utopian novel *Island*. Huxley, who had done so much to first bring psychedelics to the attention of the larger culture, described how this utopian community used what they called a *moksha* medicine. *Moksha* is a Sanskrit term meaning "liberation," as the goal of yogic practices. The psychedelic *moksha* medicine was used in this utopian community during transition rituals for adolescents, for adults in transition crises, and for preparation for the dying.

The aged philosopher put his vision into practice when he was dying, of throat cancer, on the same day that President Kennedy was assassinated – November 22, 1963. His wife Laura, who was a professional musician, has related how at a certain point, suffering from extreme debilitating discomfort, he seemed to know his time was coming and he asked her to give him an injection of 100 micrograms of LSD. A second dose of 100 mcg was given a short while later. While the Dallas murder drama was unfolding on a TV set in another room, she described how his breathing, which had been labored, became easy, his expression, which had been agitated, became serene and peaceful. Her soothing voice guided him into a deeper and deeper meditative state, urging him to release all struggle and attachment into ultimate peace. The following is an extract from a letter Laura Huxley wrote to Aldous' brother Julian, his wife and a couple of close confidants. It has been published on the *Erowid* website, as part of the Myron Stolaroff collection.

After half an hour, the expression on his face began to change a little, and I asked him if he felt the effect of LSD, and he indicated no. Yet, I think that something had taken place already...the expression of his face was beginning to look as it did every time that he had the moksha medicine, when this immense expression of complete bliss and love would come over him... He was very quiet now; he was very quiet and his legs were getting colder; higher and higher I could see purple areas of cyanosis. Then I began to talk to him, saying "Light and free." Some of these thing I told him at night in these last few weeks before he would go to sleep, and now I said it more convincingly, more intensely - "go, go, let go, darling; forward and up. You are going forward and up; you are going towards the light. Willing and consciously you are going, willingly and consciously, and you are doing this beautifully; you are doing this so beautifully - you are going towards the light; you are going towards a greater love; you are going forward and up. It is so easy; it is so beautiful. You are doing it so beautifully, so easily. Light and free. Forward and up. You are going towards Maria's love with my love. You are going towards a greater love than you have ever known. You are going towards the best, the greatest love, and it is easy, it is so easy, and you are doing it so beautifully."

I was very, very near his ears, and I hope I spoke clearly and understandingly. Once I asked him, "Do you hear me?" He squeezed my hand. He was hearing me...Later on I asked the same question, but the hand didn't move any more. Now from two o'clock until the time he died, which was five-twenty, there was complete peace except for once. That must have been about three-thirty or four, when I saw the beginning of struggle in his lower lip. His lower lip began to move as if it were going to be a struggle for air. Then I gave the direction even more forcefully...The twitching of the lower lip lasted only a little bit, and it seemed to respond completely to what I was saying...The twitching stopped, the breathing became slower and slower, and there was absolutely not the slightest indication of contraction, of struggle. It was just that the breathing became slower - and slower - and slower, and at five-twenty the breathing stopped.

I had been warned in the morning that there might be some up-setting convulsions towards the end, or some sort of contraction of the lungs, and noises. People had been trying to prepare me for some horrible physical reaction that would probably occur. None of this happened, actually the ceasing of the breathing was not a drama at all, because it was done so slowly, so gently, like a piece of music just finishing *sempre piu piano dolcemente*... There was not the feeling that with the last breath, the spirit left. It had just been gently leaving for the last four hours...These five people all said that this was the most serene, the most beautiful death. Both doctors and nurse said they had never seen a person in similar physical condition going off so completely without pain and without struggle.

Mythic guides and guardians of the land of the dead

The mythology of most cultures know a figure variously known as the guide of souls (Gk: *psychopompos*) or angel of death, who comes from the spirit world to assist and guide the soul on this ultimate journey into the unknown. This figure sometimes takes on the fearful associations of the dying process itself, as in the folkloric image of the "grim reaper," mercilessly cutting down human lives, regardless of status, beauty or wealth. In shamanistic cultures, the living shaman may invoke his or her special spirit animals, be it Raven, Wolf or another, when it comes time to escort someone to the otherworld. Especially the owl, with its superior night-time vision, was regarded as an excellent guide – as related in the novel of Kwakiutl life by Margaret Craven, *I Heard the Owl Call My Name.*

The gifted psychic Kurt Leland, in his book *The Unanswered Question,* which is a kind of ecology of the after-life realm, distinguishes between spirits he calls *facilitators,* who are "taking a break from the incarnational cycle" to guide us through the after-death zone; and those he calls *overseers*, who "are no longer focused on the human life-cycle and guide us in our spiritual evolution." These overseers are probably equivalent to what other writings call *ascended masters* or *bodhisattvas.*

The medieval Jewish mystical tradition speaks of the angel *Lailah*, whose name means "Night," who is both the midwife of souls destined to be conceived and born, and also the escort for souls that are dying and returning to the heavenly home from which they originated. According to the *midrashim* "Lailah is a guardian angel who watches over us all of our days. And when the time has come to take leave of this world, it is Lailah who leads us to the World to Come." Another mythic figure associated with dying is *Azrael,* who is revered as an Angel of Death in Islamic mysticism but also known in the Hebrew biblical traditions, where he has more fearful and negative associations.

In Greek myth, different figures personify the benign spiritual and the horrible physical aspects of death. *Hermes* the divine messenger was the guide who stood by the souls as they embarked on the river crossing to the Underworld of Hades, showing them the way. *Thanatos* was the dark–robed *daimon* who personified the release from the body, like his twin brother *Hypnos*, sleep. And *Kharon* (or *Charon*) was the rough and unkempt ferryman, with fiercely flashing eyes, who pushed and beat reluctant passengers on to his boat to cross the foul and murky waters of the river *Styx* (whose name means "pain"). Souls had to be prepared to pay the ferryman for this river crossing – and hence it was a funerary custom to place a coin on the deceased person's mouth, or two coins on the eye-lids. Souls that couldn't pay for the passage, i.e. who died unattended or unprepared, were likely to wander listlessly about before being able to complete the crossing to the other side.

The crossing of the river Styx as well as sometimes the swampy river called *Acheron* (whose name means "sorrow"), was only the first phase of the journey. Then, at the entrance to the gates of Hades, souls encounter the ferocious, three-headed dog *Cerberus* (Gk: *Kerberos),* who eats only live flesh. Thus, once the human souls no longer have their fleshly body, they cannot return to their former life. Perhaps the flesh-eating, three-headed Kerberos symbolizes how the ravages of old age, disease or fatal wounds may devour the upper, middle and lower parts of the body at the time of dying.

In the Egyptian myth of the underworld passage, called *Dwat*, a somewhat similar role to that of the dog Kerberos is played by *Ammit*, the crocodile-dog. Portrayed in numerous temple paintings, he sits by the throne of Osiris, Lord of the Underworld, and waits while the goddess *Maat* weighs each human heart against her feather of truth. Souls that answer truthfully to the questions posed by the Forty-two Assessors, can pass on to the higher regions, but the hearts weighed down with falsehoods are devoured by Ammit, and those souls go into some kind of purgatory or rehabilitation program.

The myths of Cerberus the dog and Ammit the hybrid crocodile-dog are related to the widespread cross-cultural shamanic theme of dismemberment as a preliminary to being re-constituted (re-membered) for healing and liberation. The difference between the two is that the Graeco-Roman Cerberus symbolizes more the devouring destruction of the physical body, while the Egyptian Ammit crocodile is focused on the elimination of the *persona* masks based on false pretenses, deceit and lies.

Tibetan Buddhist teachings on death and the afterlife

The original *Bardo Thödol*, or *Tibetan Book of the Dead*, is attributed to the legendary 8th century Indian Buddhist adept Padmasambhava, who brought Buddhism to Tibet. There are three *bardo* states described in the *Bardo Thödol* as occurring between death and rebirth; and there are three additional *bardo* states, mentioned in appended *Root Verses*, that occur between birth and death – waking life, dreaming and meditating. (I discuss these in-life *bardo* states in my book *MindSpace and TimeStream*.)

The *Bardo Thödol* concerns itself with providing guidance for the dying person on how to find their way through the after-death *bardo* states, giving detailed and explicit instructions how people can be helped to make the most favorable kind of rebirth possible. According to Tibetan Buddhism, both yogic practitioners and ordinary people with no particular yogic aptitude, can be helped to find their way through the confusing and terrifying afterlife states.

The *Book of Liberation through Understanding the Bardo States* (as it is called) teaches that liberation from the *samsaric* round of conditioned existence can occur *in*, or *from*, any of the *bardo* states, if we recognize the *bardo* state we are in, and choose the most enlightened conscious option available to us. It is for this reason that Buddhist teachers refer to it not only as a book of preparation for dying, but really a profound guidebook for both living and dying.

The teachings of the *Bardo Thödol*, in outline, are that immediately at death, in the *bardo of the moment of dying*, the dying person is urged to maintain one-pointed concentration on the "clear light," also referred to as "the uncreated." In the *Root Verses* appended to the *Bardo Thödol* the essential teaching related to each of the *bardo* states is summarized. Here is (my version of) the Root Verse for the *bardo of dying*, which emphasizes paying attention to releasing one's attachments to the physical body and world.

> *Now as the bardo of dying dawns upon me,*
> *I will abandon desires and cravings for worldly objects.*
> *Entering without distraction into the clarity of the teachings,*
> *I will merge my awareness into the space of the uncreated.*
> *The time has come to let go this body of flesh and blood --*
> *It is merely a temporary and illusory shell.*

Most ordinary people are not able to concentrate, get caught in fear and confusion and enter then into the second phase, called the *bardo of the experiencing of reality*, in which there are heavenly and hellish visions of "peaceful and wrathful deities," depicted in the fantastic iconography of Tibetan Buddhism. The deceased is repeatedly reminded, by the attendant lama-priests, not to be overwhelmed by either the heavenly or the hellish visions, but to remember that they are all projections of one's own mind. Due to lack of training and/or preparation on the part of most ordinary people, the *bardo*-traveling soul, after repeatedly lapsing into unconsciousness, then finds itself in the third phase, the *bardo of seeking rebirth,* in which he or she wanders about seeking to orient again to ordinary existence and find a family to be born into. We shall return to a discussion of the second and third *bardo* phases in the following chapters.

Four

Life Between Lives

In the Irish-Celtic tradition and also in the 19th century theosophical conception of the after-death realm, there is the notion of *Summerland* as a kind of peaceful and beautiful transitional resting and recovery place – especially valuable for those who were dying from a body racked with pain and illness. In classical Greece, the name *Elysium* or the *Elysian Fields* conveyed a similar imagery of peaceful natural scenery where the souls of the virtuous can rest. The essence of *Summerland* is that it is a resting ground where souls can reflect on the life they led, see if they learned the lesson they had intended on learning, and then try again in due course. This Summerland is not seen as a place of judgment, but rather of spiritual self-evaluation where a soul is able to review its life and gain an understanding of the total impact its actions had on the world. It was said that the ecology and geography of Summerland is an amalgam of your religious beliefs and your personal dreams and visions.

In the modern autobiographical literature on NDE (near-death experience), we can recognize some of the same Elysian Fields or Summerland imagery of a peaceful, beautiful transitional resting place, after the terrors and pains of dying. A consistent theme in the NDE accounts is that after an abrupt separation from the physical body and an OBE (out-of-body) perspective on the death scene (such as in an auto accident or during surgery), there is a profound change to a mood of painless peace and awareness of brilliant light – sometimes an entry into a tunnel with light at the end. The individual experiences the light itself as intelligent, emotionally soothing and personally welcoming.

> The last thing I remember was my doctor's assistant standing by my bed and then I left my body, and I could see it down below on the bed. I don't know how long I stayed above my body looking down at it, but suddenly I was in the most beautiful Golden Light, and I stayed there. I felt so loved, calm, peaceful, happy…the Golden light was all around me, all within me. I was in the Golden Light with no separation whatsoever…Such powerful love, and so much love, so much beauty there. I felt love, compassion, understanding, knowledge (Ring, K. *Lessons from the Light*, p. 34).

> The light was round and it did get bigger and bigger very fast, so I could have been zooming through a tunnel…I was a little scared when the light first zoomed to me (or me to it), even though it didn't hurt my eyes like I thought it would. In fact the more I looked at it, the more mesmerized I became with peacefulness…I clearly and instantly knew the light was not just a light but was ALIVE! It had a personality and was intelligence beyond comprehension…I knew the light was a being. I also knew the light being was God and was genderless (Ring, K. *op.cit.* p. 44).

The intelligent light emanation may be accompanied or followed by the appearance of previously deceased family members, like parents, ancestors or loved ones. The individual may also see angelic, spiritual beings, who telepathically convey messages of total acceptance, wisdom and peace.

> There was a light toward the end of the tunnel but before I could reach it, two figures appeared outlined in light. They communicated with me through my mind, telepathically. I recognized one of the figures as being my father. He confirmed and agreed with everything conveyed by his companion who seemed to have great authority, like an angel or one of God's helpers (Ring, K. *The Omega Project*. p. 101).

> "God" was within this brightness. I felt loved beyond all judgment…and completely accepted. This "God" communicated to me – no words, just kind of pushed knowledge into me – that I had a rough past but he/she

was delighted at my handling of my life, and that I was OK...The God was gentle, but I knew I had to go back (Ring, K. *op. cit*, p. 103).

Many of the accounts of NDEs report a sense of some kind of life-review council, in which the positive and negative features of the life are seen and evaluated. The accounts agree that the life-review process, in the company of a council of guides, elders and sometimes ancestors, is carried out in an atmosphere of loving kindness and compassion, without even a hint of punitive judgment. The deceased soul him or herself participates in this life-review – which has the quality of a shared evaluation of progress made or not made, and the lessons learned or not learned, in the life that just ended, and always in the context of total loving acceptance.

> Scenes from my life began to pass before my eyes at super high speeds. It seemed as if I was a passive observer in the process, and it was as if someone else was running the projector. I was looking at my life objectively for the first time ever. I saw the good as well as the bad (Ring, K. *Lessons from the Light*, p. 13).

> It proceeded to show me every single event in my twenty-two years of life, in a kind of instant three-dimensional panoramic review...The brightness showed me every second of all those years, in exquisite detail, in what seemed only an instant of time. As I relived my life, there was no judgment being placed on it by anyone. No one pointed a finger at the horrors, or blamed me for any of my mistakes. There was only the overwhelming presence of complete acceptance, total openness, and deepest love (Ring, K. *op. cit*. p. 165).

These encounters and after-death visions occur in a realm completely outside of time – indeed the whole NDE experience often lasts only a few minutes, as measured in real or clock-time – although they may take hours or many written pages to describe afterwards. The complete transcendence of time in the after-death realm was dramatically illustrated by the experience of a man who had an unexpected NDE while under the influence of LSD. This story was told to me by a witness of this occurrence.

The man in question had taken a fairly high dose of LSD, together with some friends, at night, on the rooftop of an apartment building in Detroit. On the roof were some ventilator shafts, about two to three feet in height above the rest of the roof. In the profound absorption of his LSD-induced trance, as the man stepped off the ventilator shaft on which he was standing, he *thought* he had stepped off the edge of the roof, and was therefore about to die. In the *second or less* which it took for him to "fall" down the two or three feet, a quick succession of scenes from his life flashed before his astonished eyes (Metzner, R. *The Unfolding Self,* p. 144).

The complete transcendence of time as in this account is found in many accounts of NDEs and especially the life review. The NDE researcher Kenneth Ring has suggested that in such experiences, *time is spatialized.* He cites the following account of a woman who had an NDE as a child and another one as an adult.

With regard to the question of time, everything happened instantaneously. The whole thing happened all at once but we are bound by the restraints of language. …When my life went before my eyes, it was not from my earliest memory of thirteen months. There was an enormous TV screen in front of me. … Way over on the left was my memory at thirteen months, and way over on the right was memory at thirty-eight. Everything in between was right there and I could see the whole thing, all at the same instant (Ring, K. *Lessons from the Light,* p. 150).

Some devout or fundamentalist Christians who have experienced NDEs report a sense of compassionate revelation of the truth of one's life – not the punitive separation of "sheep" and "goats," nor condemnation to eternal punishment or long-term purgatory, found in fundamentalist dogma. Indeed, in the NDE account of a devout Catholic, she mentions that she first resisted the angelic guide visions due to her mortal terror of "dying in sin," until she was finally able to take in the compassionate acceptance of the saintly figure who appeared to her.

The recognition of an after-death meeting with compassionate guides and supportive ancestors can also occur in the context of past-life therapy, where it can be immensely liberating.

A woman-physician of my acquaintance had repeated disturbing visions, in dreams and altered states of consciousness, of being pursued by a raving mob of men and women, armed with sticks and pitch-forks, who screamed "kill the witch, kill the witch." The visions always ended with her running, alone and terrified, and the screaming mob running after her. I guided her, in a therapeutic trance-state, to stop running, turn around and face the mob. Immediately, she knew and accepted that it was a past-life dying memory. As she lifted off from her body, she was met and welcomed with love by her mother and aunt, fellow wise woman healers who had died before her.

The fear associated with traumatic deaths may function to fixate the memory of the trauma, causing it to carry over into the next life – in much the same way that traumas lead to compulsive repetitions within one life-time. For the reincarnated "witch," the attack visions did not recur.

Communication between the living and the spirits of the dead

In the 19th and early 20th centuries, in the West, the inherent spiritual need for communication between the living and their deceased loved ones was afforded through psychically gifted spiritual mediums. One of the most astonishing was Emily French (1831-1912), a frail, deaf woman in Rochester, NY, who in her consultations, manifested the very loud, male voice of her Indian guide "Red Jacket," in what was called "direct-independent voice communication" – that gave detailed and elaborate answers to questions about the after-life. Her teachings, which were researched and recorded at the time by the attorney Edward Randall, have recently been re-issued in a fascinating compilation by N. Riley Heagerty called *The French Revelation*.

To my mind, one of the most fascinating insights from this work is their account of the role of mediumship or "spirit sugges-tion," as it was also called, in the creation of works of literature and art. The authorship of the works of William Shakespeare, so brilliant in their diversity and their understanding of the human psyche and their knowledge of the ways of many cultures and times, has often been disputed. How did this working class, simple country fellow and actor come up with these extaordinary works? In the book *The French Revelation*, the spirit-authors chanelling through Emily French and Edward Randall, are quoted as asserting that —

> All the Shakespearean works were, beyond a doubt, the product of his pen, but the conceptions, the plays, the tragedies were the work of many minds, given Shakespeare by spirit suggestion. He was the sensitive instrument through which a group of learned and distinguished scholars, inhabitants of many lands when in earth-life, gave to posterity the sublime masterpieces of the Bard of Avon. (The full text of their discussion of Shakespeare is given in the Appendix)

It is perhaps a sign of a change in the collective consciousness in Western society that in the period since the World War II, there has been a notable increase in documented, verifiable communications between the living and the dead – unmediated by a third person. Contemporary gifted psychics such as Kurt Leland and Sylvia Browne have also contributed to the literature describing the after-death realms, as have hypnotherapists such as Michael Newton, who has specialized in deep trance inductions that take people to the life between lives.

In dreams and visionary encounters with the spirits of the dead, people have often remarked that when they did finally overcome their grief and guilt enough to be receptive to the loved one, they appeared, not in the aged, diseased or crippled form of the time of death, but in the prime of life, healthy and glowing. It is my sense that such visions of a rejuvenated form may appear when some time has elapsed since the dying – and the deceased soul will have gone through some kind of healing and purifying adjustment to life on the other side. It may also be that the survivor needs to have come to terms with their grief (and sometimes residual guilt at not having done enough for the deceased), to be receptive to such visionary encounters.

In his book *ReUnions – Visionary Encounters with Departed Loved Ones,* the psychiatrist Raymond Moody, who was one of the first to investigate NDEs, describes his pioneering research with what he calls a *psychomanteum,* a specially created room with a tilted mirror, that can facilitate visions and conversations with the souls of the dead. The dead generally appeared healthy and spoke in a kind but firm manner, educating their survivor loved ones about the reality of life in the spirit world, often encouraging them to get on with their life. Sometimes the subjects will meet a different deceased family member than the one they expected or hoped for.

> I had not really been planning to meet up with my nephew while I was there in the apparition room. I sat there for what seemed like a long period of time…All of a sudden I stopped trying to force it and just sat back and relaxed… This is when I suddenly had a very strong sense of the presence of my nephew, who had committed suicide. I was close to this nephew, who was named after my father and me. There was this very strong sense of his presence and I heard his voice very clearly. He was talking to me. He greeted me and he brought me a very simple message. He said, "Let my mother know that I am fine and that I love her very much." The experience was very profound. I know he was there with me. I didn't see anything, but I had a very strong sense of him and his presence. This voice is different from just having a thought, and it is not exactly like the regular experience of hearing a voice. It is like being spoken to mentally…I feel sure that I was in communication with my nephew (Moody, R., *ReUnions,* p. 91-92).

Moody reported several general observations from his research with this mode of after-death communication. One was that people often encountered a different deceased family member than the one they expected. Another was that the apparitions, when they did appear, could also leave the mirror and stand near the subject. Some people even felt touched or hugged by their relative in spirit form– though with others, touching was expressly discouraged. Although Moody had not expected it, in about half the cases actual conversations took place, usually of a reassuring and clarifying nature, sometimes with the actual hearing of a voice, other times more directly telepathic.

Moody and others in the psychomanteum received the impression from such encounters that there was some difficulty involved for the deceased souls in making themselves visible to the living, and yet all the subject insisted emphatically that the re-unions were with the "real" persons – not fantasies or imaginary – and the experience was spiritually transformative, changing forever the survivor's outlook on the meaning of life and death.

After my son Ari died, it was more than ten years before I was able to dissolve enough of the grief and guilt to be able to have meaningful conversations with him, in a waking meditative state. These conversations did not however involve my "seeing" his form (which would occur spontaneously only in dreams – usually in the form of memory images). Most often our communications were a kind of subtle inner "hearing" where I would ask him a question and then directly receive a response.

One time, an unexpected communication took place: I was sitting meditating in my room, when I suddenly clearly heard a child's voice say "Dad." At first I thought it was my daughter, but I knew she was not in the house. Then I thought it was my step-son – but I realized it couldn't be him, since he didn't call me "Dad." So then I realized that it was Ari, trying to get my attention and initiate a conversation. He proceeded to encourage me, just with telepathic thought-transfer, to talk about the myths of Odin and his son Baldur, in the talks I was planning to give on an upcoming trip to Germany. I had been reluctant to do so, because those stories touched me almost too close to home.

After I had read Raymond Moody's book *Re-Unions,* when I was on a vision quest in the California Desert, I inwardly asked Ari if he would show himself so I could "see" him, as people did in the psychomanteum. His response was immediate and it seemed to enter my mind from a place right next to my heart – "what do you want to know – I'm right here?" His response confirmed my impression that manifesting a visual apparition was indirect and somewhat difficult for those in the Spirit World. Their preferred mode of communicating appears to be a kind of telepathic communion with direct thought-transfer.

Another mode of facilitated therapeutic communication with the deceased was unexpectedly discovered by the psychologist Allan Botkin, in the course of working with traumatized war veterans at a Veterans Administration clinic in Chicago. Botkin was using the EMDR (eye-movement desensitization and reprocessing) method to assist Vietnam and Iraq war veterans in healing from PTSD reactions. The EMDR procedure, in which the client is instructed to follow the horizontal hand-movements of the therapist with his eyes, while recalling horrific trauma scenes, has a proven track record of success in alleviating trauma reactions.

Some of the soldiers who had witnessed or caused another's death (a fellow soldier or civilian), suddenly found themselves in an encounter with the soul of the dead – and a communication of forgiveness and peaceful healing. Allan Botkin, who was as surprised as his veteran clients at discovering the reality of post-mortem consciousness and communication, has described his method and results in his book *Induced After Death Communication.*

The following post-mortem conversation between a man and his 22-year-old son who was killed in a street-gang assault, was related to me by the father, who was a client of mine and a friend. I had shown him how to establish a communication ritual with his deceased son by entering into a calm meditative state in a peaceful setting. I suggested he record the answers he received in writing. The father first asked to know what the dying process was like for his son. He got the following reply:

> I was alone for a little while. Confused; wondering what happened. I saw light, went toward it. I was met; I was warm, bathed in love. I felt sure again; I knew where I was. There were people I love, all taking care of me, helping with the shock. They held me. I just took it all in. It was like sitting in the kitchen with you guys. Safe, familiar, just being cared for, people paying attention to what I needed right then. I was alright very soon. My soul still hurt for a while from what happened. The violence. The loss. Not being able to go home to my girl-friend. But I was alright.

The father then asked what the transition is usually like and what happens in the process. The reply clearly shows that the dead son's soul picked up on the living father's own anxiety about dying and responded to it with compassion and reassurance.

> Disorientation, disconnection. Seeing things from above. Un-tethered. Then something guides you and there's a sense of direction. A place or some distant point beckoning. Like a lighthouse in the night. Then you are greeted. It depends on what you need who shows up. If you were really broken by your life, some healers come. They take you in hand, shower you with love. Caress you – yes, you still get caressed here. Then you go on to the familiar ones. Soon. And then you know everything's alright. You're home. It didn't take long for me. You're more afraid, so you might need a bit more caressing, being taken care of. We'll see. But you'll be alright. We'll be here waiting. I'll be here. Don't worry. It'll be fine. We'll pull you through the hole.

In such communicative exchanges, as indicated earlier, the deceased typically appear to be radiantly healthy, and convey perspectives of expanded understanding. This kind of communication occurred for me in an extremely vivid dream I had exactly one year after my mother had died. Sleeping in my home in California, my dreaming self saw my mother lying in the London funeral home where I had seen her when she died. As I gazed at her face I was struck, again, by the contrast between the cherished familiarity of the features and their absolute stillness – so different from their constant motion when she was alive. As I was contemplating this paradox, her face changed suddenly to that of a radiantly beautiful young woman – who opened her eyes and smiled at me. At that instant, there was a distinct *pop* in my brain, dissolving and releasing the thought-form I had been unconsciously holding of "that old lady my mother," and reminding me of her immortal essence-soul.

The life-review in Egyptian after-death teachings

In the complex after-death teachings of pharaonic Egypt, which date back to a far-earlier time than either the Greek myths or the Christian teachings, we can recognize certain elements that were taken up by these later traditions. We saw already in the last chapter, how Ammit the crocodile-dog, situated near the throne of Osiris, Lord of the Underworld, devours the residues of evil and deceitful actions in the physical body – in much the same way as the hell-hound Cerberus devours the fleshly remains of the deceased.

In numerous Egyptian temple paintings, we can see the post-mortem meeting with *Osiris*, the Lord of the Underworld, portrayed. In Egyptian mythology, Osiris has three forms – green, black and white. In his green-skinned form he is the vegetation god, from whose body lying on the ground, the nourishing grain sprouts upward. In his black skin-robe, he is the god of fertility, consort of Isis the Black Goddess, associated with the rich black earth of the River Nile when it has flooded the land. The black color was associated in ancient Egypt, and in the cultures of Old Europe, with life and fertility; and not with death, as in the later Indo-European (including Greek, Germanic and Celtic) cultures. The White Goddess on the other hand, and the white-robed Osiris, were associated with death and symbolized in sculptured figurines of marble or bone.

In the Egyptian view of the after-death journey, the soul of the deceased is accompanied by the ibis-headed deity *Thoth*, the wise and incorruptible record-keeper of the gods, who has recorded all of the good and bad deeds of the deceased. It was the role of Thoth to present the soul of the deceased with the scenes of the life-review, clearly and objectively registering the good and bad deeds – as has been reported in NDEs in modern times.

The soul of the deceased is also accompanied by the falcon-headed *Horus* and the black jackal (or jackal-headed) *Anubis*, who was the patron deity of healers and doctors and those in charge of the mummification process.

After being escorted by Anubis, Horus and Thoth to stand in front of the white-robed Osiris, the heart of the deceased was weighed against the feather of truth in the scales of the goddess *Maat*. The deceased had to answer, truthfully, the questions posed by the *Forty-two Assessors* – who are also painted on the tomb walls, seated in rows.

The questions were posed in such a way that if you falsely denied having done impure, unjust or selfish things, each falsehood would add to the weight of your heart. The heart heavy with falsehood went into a realm where its toxic impurities were devoured by Ammit the crocodile-dog. If you answered truthfully all the questions, your heart would stay balanced with the feather of truth – and you would be able to pass on to the bright road to the realm of the stars and the high deities.

Joan Grant (1907-1989) was a psychically gifted English woman who has written six posthumous autobiographies, based on her detailed recall of her past lives. In *Winged Pharaoh* she describes an Egyptian life in which she was both priestess and queen and underwent painstaking training in what was called "far memory." She describes the pharaonic dying ritual and going through the after-death experience, the weighing of the heart and the questioning by the forty-two assessors. Here, for example, are five of the questions (as she transcribed them):

> And the first shall challenge him, saying: Hast thou treated thy body wisely and considerately, even as thy creator cherished thee in the days of thy youth?
> And the fourth shall say: Hast thou lain only with the woman whom they spirit loveth also?
> And the thirteenth shall say: Hath thine heart been untorn by the claws of jealousy?
> And the twenty-third shall say: Hast thou given bread to

the poor and the fruits of thy vineyards to the weary?
And the fortieth shall say: Hast thou remembered the plants, which were once thy brothers, and quenched their thirst and tended them so that they flourished?

The teaching of this mythic image from ancient Egypt represents, in some ways, a prefiguration of the judgement scene portrayed in later Christian iconography. However, in its depiction of an impartial assessment or evaluation by a council of beings (rather than a dualistic judgement of good vs sinful and subsequent punishment), and the emphasis on truth-telling, it more closely resembles the reported experiences of NDEs.

We cannot of course know for sure what we will encounter in the *Hereafter*. Perhaps the Egyptian teachings, and the reports of NDEs, were all based on the experience of spiritually developed people – and the experience of ordinary, unprepared people is different.

The second bardo in the Tibetan Buddhist after-death teachings

In the *Bardo Thödol*, the deceased, if not able to pass on to the unobstructed, pure land realms, during the *bardo of dying*, due to insufficient concentration and preparation, wanders through the "intermediate realms" of the second *bardo* realm. In this phase the dominant feature are dramatically contrasting visionary encounters with peaceful, angelic beings and ferocious, demonic ones. There are encounters with "knowledge-holding deities" – whose flame-surrounded bodies burn off the false images obstructing and distorting true knowledge.

The deceased is repeatedly reminded, by the attendant lamas, not to be overly attracted by the heavenly or frightened by the hellish visions. These beautiful and ugly visions, he is told, are the reflections and projections of your mind and life, as seen in the mirror held up by the death god *Yama*. If you stay centered in the middle path between the extremes of dualistic judgment, you will still be able to pass through to the pure light realms of the higher dimensions.

Here is the encapsulated teaching, from the *Root Verses* concerning this second after-death phase, which the Evans-Wentz translation calls the "*bardo* of experiencing reality." Since it deals essentially with the heaven-and-hell visions that one may encounter in this phase, I am calling it the *bardo of visions*.

> *Now as I enter into the bardo of visions,*
> *I will abandon all awe and terror that arises.*
> *Recognizing whatever appears as my own thought-forms,*
> *As apparitions and visions in this intermediate state.*
> *This is a crucial turning-point on the path.*
> *I will not fear the peaceful and terrifying visions in my mind.*

However, due to lack of training and/or preparation on the part of most ordinary people, the *bardo* traveler, after repeatedly lapsing into unconsciousness due to lack of concentration and fear, then finds himself in the third phase, the *bardo of seeking rebirth*, in which he wanders about seeking to orient himself again to ordinary existence. We shall discuss this rebirth phase further in the next chapter.

The council of ancestral souls and guiding spirits

The modern traveler into the after-death realms, whether in meditative, psychedelic or NDE states, is probably unlikely to encounter figures from Egyptian, Tibetan Buddhist or any other mythology unless he or she has specifically, through prior interest or training, cultivated a connection to these deities and recognizes them by their appearance. To my mind, in the earlier part of my life, these figures were constructions of the mythic imagination. However, after many years of study of these ancient cultures and explorations in meditative, shamanic and entheogenic states of consciousness, some of these figures have at times assumed a certain vividness and unmistakable reality.

The reality-recognition involved in such visionary encounters is not unlike that of a dream vision in which you recognize a deceased member of your family or a friend. You may come to realize that the dream encounter with your deceased ancestor or loved one is not a fantasy construction, but a real encounter with a real being – now existing only in the spirit world. While we do of course create all kinds of fantasy beings in our imagination and our dreams, it may also happen that we encounter spirit beings we call *guides* or *deities* with an unmistakeable air of reality, and that we receive teachings and guidance from them with direct relevance to our lives.

In my book *The Well of Remembrance*, I related how in the course of working on the stories of the Norse gods, I several times had the distinct impression that the insights and understandings I was receiving were coming to me from *Odin*, the knowledge-seeking shaman god of the ancient Germanic people – whose mythology I was researching. After several journeys to Egypt and intensive immersion in Egyptian death-rebirth teachings, I unexpectedly received a visionary confirmation of the reality of *Anubis*.

> I was guiding, while seated, a small group of travelers lying in two rows in what we call our "spirit canoe" on a deep, inner space journey. I was leaning over to one side, to lay a comforting hand on one of the travelers who was weeping, when I suddenly became aware, out of the corner of my eye, of a large black dog sitting next to me, on the other side. I was simultaneously startled by the enormous size of the black dog, which reached as far as my shoulders and immediately calmed by the realization that the spirit-dog was perfectly still and emanating an atmosphere of peace and protection. Then I realized, with awe and gratitude, that Anubis had in fact appeared to assist and guide us in our meditations on the after-death journey – just as he would have, perhaps, to the priests of Anubis ministering to the initiates in pharaonic Egypt.

In our divination work on connecting with the ancestors from the prenatal phase, as described in Chapter Two, we have sometimes found other, higher-dimensional spirit beings together with the council of ancestors. In other divinations, I may guide people directly to a council of souls that includes ancestral souls and also higher-dimensional spirit guides or divinities from a realm far beyond the ordinary earthly human world, but connected to us in a spiritual way. With continuing meditative attunements to these soul dimensions, people may begin to identify and name particular beings who guide us across many life-times.

The man who, in a prenatal divination (see Chapter One, p. 22) remembered the painful rupture between his parents immediately after his birth, said that, when guided to the council of souls –

> I kept getting images of other beings, Spirit beings whom I had connected with before. I did recognize them from previous sessions. And they were back again, they were light beings. They weren't human. And it was about an agreement I made with them…before they would answer my questions about what was my purpose here, in this incarnation. It was very clear. And there was a celebration, when I remembered that agreement with the soul

council. It was to live my truth with integrity and be that light being that I am – open and loving… in service.

In a parental reconciliation divination, a woman psychiatrist was reviewing her fateful karmic connection with her mother, and getting the guidance from her ancestors to look for her destiny beyond that relationship. Following that guidance, she found herself in a higher council of elders beyond or behind the ancestors.

> I am dissolving, until only essence or soul is left. Behind the council of ancestral souls I find myself with a higher council of elders, and a vision of an order behind the order. At this point absolute freedom arises from the acceptance of that which is. I can see these orders graphically and see this higher order in the connections between the planets. I am seeing what happens when a soul chooses a human incarnation. I'm seeing how the human soul enters into the cells, how it expresses itself, and how parental qualities give that expression a distinctive character. I see how I've received everything from my parents and how the soul then expresses that which it is my destiny to bring into expression.
>
> From there I arrive at a state in which all oppositions fall together, yet it is not some kind of homogenous mush. I recognize the holistic principle of body-soul-oneness. I recognize that in the last resort there is only one Great Soul, from which I emerge and into which I return. The soul has an "ego" – she is that ego, but not in the psychoanalytic sense, but in the sense that she has that indivisible, unchanging identity, which incarnates into different bodies. The incarnation is chosen through the ordering principle.

I have come to understand that this soul council, made up of ancestral souls and guiding spirits, is our support and guiding team throughout our life and in the worlds beyond. The souls of our genetic ancestors can assist us with their knowledge of our personal, familial antecedents – in the society and in the times in which we live. With the council of elders and guides we become aware that we have soul connections that span many life-times in many worlds and they may give us teachings relating to our life purpose, karma and destiny.

In the following account a man relates how the council of elders and ancestors helped him to see the karmic negativity in his ancestral lineage and guided him to choose not to continue that line, by not having children.

> When I went to my father's side, my great mentors were always my grandparents…For whatever reason, all the kids that they had were probably actually crazy. So I stood before them and communicated to them that I was where the buck stopped, that I wasn't continuing the lineage. To which my grandmother and my grandfather smiled and my dad really blew up. Because I think they knew that it had produced a lot of real craziness. For me, the insanity is when you go out and kill people and do property damage and be damaged and this inability to manage sanity…So that was really good.
>
> I realized that I came from a lineage of warriors and warlocks and berserkers, who came to disrupt humanity, to cause change, to develop honor, courage and lessons of sacrifice and compassion, and to turn the earth up on it's edge, to turn humanity on it's side and to have the kind of expansion and contraction that would cause humanity to grow out of it in a very powerful way or to totally self-destruct and not waste any more time. I have been experiencing a shift into that warrior heart. In discovering that lineage it was really fulfilling because I had been at odds with having been a warrior. I had been at odds with having killed so many people, and I had been at odds with having been killed so many times. I was more conscious and aware of being last night than, perhaps, in any other sitting over these past twenty five or thirty years. I was just ecstatic.
>
> I realized that I have nothing to say about how the world is and I have everything to say about how I interpret or how I've framed the world. That really doesn't give me much power to go down the path of pessimism. There really is a developing plan and a developing humanity and that in my role or my intention or my purpose, as the creator of my life and of this life, is to bring myself fully to each moment and to stop turning my back and walking away when it doesn't fit my judgments or my opinions or when it doesn't go my way. I think, in short, that I had an initiation.

As we have seen, in modern hypnotic and entheogenic explorations of the after-death realms, as well as in the accounts of past-life therapists, we learn of the soul's meeting with a council of guiding spirits (or spirit guides) – a council that we meet with after a life has ended, to review and evaluate the lessons learned, and meet again as the choice is made to incarnate, to preview a new human existence.

Of course, we may also meet with them and consult with them in meditative, spiritual journeys during life – and this kind of practice is described in Eastern and Western spiritual traditions. This council, which seems to consist of about a dozen or so identifiable spirit beings, functions as a kind of guiding and support team for the myriad journeys and challenges of our life. Perhaps this council is the contemporary equivalent of the meeting with Thoth, Maat, Osiris and the Forty-two Assessors in Ancient Egypt, and the "Knowledge-Holding Deities" of the Tibetan Buddhists.

In my experience, the beings of this council convey an attitude of total acceptance, compassion and objectivity – while making clear that it is *we* who are also making the choices and evaluations. The council of ancestral and guiding spirits is not in a superior, judging position towards us – we, as souls, are members of the council and participants in its deliberations. As the *Bardo Thödol* repeatedly reminds us, the "knowledge-holding deities" are emanations of own thought forms – which doesn't mean they are fantasy constructions, but rather they exist within us in the inner dimensions of our own multi-dimensional beingness.

In one past-life regression in which I was guided by Winafred Lucas, Ph.D., a psychologist who has perhaps done more than anyone to open up to the modern mind to the reality of the spiritual dimensions, I was shown how the *life-review council* inwardly connects with the *life-preview council* for the following incarnation.

In the regression, I recalled a life as a woman in 16th or 17th century France, who was seduced, made pregnant and abandoned by an aristocratic military officer – and then shunned by family and community and condemned to a life of isolation and poverty. Immediately after reliving the release of the dying and in meeting with the life-review council, I at first wanted not to be re-born as a woman – so that henceforth I could be the one in the favored position in patriarchal society. However, as the council of guiding spirits considered the process of choosing the next life, I was shown that it would be better to not take the vengeful compensating position of becoming a dominating male – but instead to undo the curse of patriarchal conditioning which led to my misery in the life just passed. So I was guided to choose again to be born as a woman, but this time into a family and community where female and male children (and adults) were respected and cherished equally.

In the following chapter, I will discuss how the life between lives (second *bardo*) ends with the process of choosing another human incarnation. This incarnational choice then begins the phase that includes conception and the entire prenatal journey – what the *Tibetan Book of the Dead* calls the *bardo of rebirth*.

Conception, Birth, Death, and the Six *Bardo* ("In-between") States

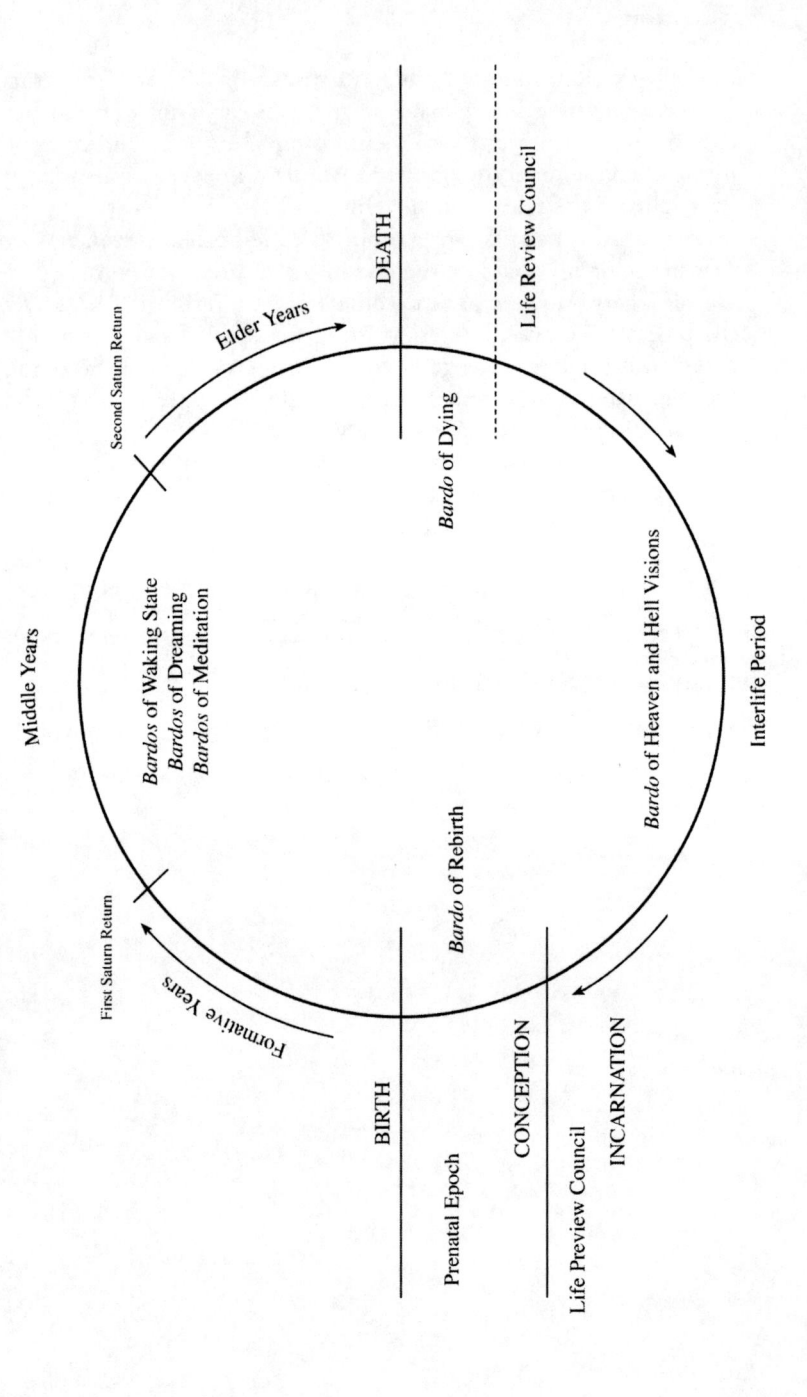

Middle Years

Second Saturn Return

Elder Years

DEATH

Life Review Council

Bardo of Dying

Bardos of Waking State
Bardos of Dreaming
Bardos of Meditation

Interlife Period

Bardo of Heaven and Hell Visions

Bardo of Rebirth

First Saturn Return

Formative Years

BIRTH

CONCEPTION

INCARNATION

Prenatal Epoch

Life Preview Council

102

Five

From Incarnation to Conception and Rebirth

I have come to believe, in accord with Asian and Western esoteric teachings on reincarnation, that the soul chooses the family and community in which to be conceived and born, with divine guidance and in accord with karmic predispositions. Sometimes, as we have seen, there may be factors of karmic connections or indebtedness that may enter into the soul's choice of ancestral family. As I described in Chapter Two, becoming conscious of the actual soul connection with the parents and the parents of the parents (and sometimes ancestors further back in the parental lineages), can be enormously healing and empowering to the individual. It can lead to a sense of having an unconditionally supportive back-up team and to a deeper knowing of one's purpose in life.

If a soul's purpose is to be a musician, he/she may choose to be born into a family where one or both of the parents (or grandparents) are themselves musicians who can nurture this particular talent. One destined to be a scientist may choose to be incarnated into a family of scientific talent and inclinations. Some souls apparently choose to be born into families of great wealth, perhaps in order to learn how to handle wealth in a way that is in accord with their spiritual purpose, without being seduced or blinded. Others may choose to be born into the hardship of poverty, perhaps to learn to overcome one's circumstances or to cultivate non-material values.

When people tune in to the place of soul communion and the life-preview council, they know, feel and sense that they have, with high spiritual awareness, *chosen* to be here, on Earth, in this particular life for a particular purpose (or purposes). This can be a life-changing realization that puts all of our other strivings, confusions and frustrations in perspective. It is the moment of choice and freedom pointed to by the famous Zen *koan: What was your original face before you were born?* In other words – in what direction were you facing, what was your original intention?

Koans are not meant to be a answered – just asked, repeatedly. This kind of asking opens us up to be receptive to the influx of knowing from inner, spiritual Source. Therefore, we may translate the koan as follows – and I suggest this self-inquiry for the reader—*What was, and is, your soul's vision for this life, this incarnation?*

When I shared an earlier version of this chapter with Buddhist philosopher, deep ecologist and friend Joanna Macy, she wrote to me that she was struck by how the section on incarnational choice resonated with one of the workshop processes she had developed.

"In *Coming Back to Life*, it's called "My Choices for this Life." I tend to call it the "Bodhisattva Check-In"...it evolved from an earlier exercise known as "The Incarnation Committee." It involves using the power of the imagination to...replay the decision to take birth as a human in the 20th century, and then stepping into the particular conditions of this last birth, understanding that they are probably just right for the mission you have come to accomplish. Given the present state of the world...he results of this process are often incredibly moving and empowering."

This place of soul communion and soul council, out of which comes the choice to incarnate, is pre-conception when seen from the perspective of ordinary linear time; hence we can get there by regressive remembering. But it is also still present now, until the end of our present incarnation; hence we can get there by direct divination, and then bring that knowing-feeling-sensing awareness "down" through the personality systems, or "inner bodies," and into the physical body (a process known as *soul infusion*).

The highly skilled medical intuitive Caroline Myss calls the agreement made between souls the *sacred contract.* She says, "a Sacred Contract is an agreement your soul makes before you are born." Sylvia Browne describes the process of choice as the designing of a *chart*, featuring major life events and circumstances in a kind of advance scenario.

There have been many different mappings of the major types of life-path a soul may choose to follow, once incarnated, conceived and born. Some, like Caroline Myss, relate the soul's purpose to which of the twelve Zodiac signs the person is born under; the Arica esoteric school uses the nine points of the ancient enneagram to define nine types of soul orientation and values; my wise friend Angeles Arrien has described a paradigm of four major "ways" (Warrior, Teacher, Healer, Visionary). In a forthcoming book in the present series I will describe six major life-paths or fields of action in society that souls may choose – concentrating on one or combining two or three or more.

In divinations to the soul council we are not so concerned with the details of the different paths, but with the process by which a person may themselves get an inner feeling, knowing or intuition about their life purpose. Actually, I've observed that often just being in communication with the soul council and knowing-feeling that one's life *has* a deeper, spiritual purpose for being here on Earth, even without any more details, can make a huge difference. It gives the person a criterion by which to decide whether a particular area, work, place, career or associate one is involved with is in accord with one's life purpose – and if it is not, to leave it, without regret or blame.

Through such divination work, I have been led to the conclusion that *souls love challenges,* apparently – they often do not choose an easy path. This is especially so when souls get to the point in their evolution where they realize that passively letting past karmic patterns determine our lives and our destiny is not a path of liberation. The Tibetan Buddhists emphasize that being born as a human being on Earth is a *precious opportunity* and we should not waste it. Perhaps this is because the greater the difficulties, the greater the learning. Any learning of anything surely involves challenges to rise above obstacles and weaknesses. How could growth take place if our lives proceeded to the tune of "roses, roses all the way?"

The Earth time-space dimension is the most restrictive and arduous of all the dimensions in which our existence unfolds. We recognize this every time we experience the dissolution of time-space and materiality when we visit the inner realms in dreams or visionary states. The difficulty stems from the fact that a human incarnation in the time-space-matter dimension is generally more or less cut-off from the awareness of its spiritual origin and essence.

This is the meaning of the teaching in the Asian spiritual traditions (both Hindu and Buddhist) that the default condition of the human being at birth is un-consciousness or non-consciousness (*avidya*). This Sanskrit term, literally "not-knowing," and sometimes misleadingly translated as "ignorance" or "delusion," refers to the non-consciousness by the newborn infant of their true spiritual origin, as a soul, a child of divine parentage.

The soul, all three souls (of mother, father and child) know, at that level, that once we are conceived in a fleshly womb and then born into the time-space world of earthly conditions – all bets are off, so to speak. Everything, all knowledge of our origin and mission, may be forgotten, even the existence of the soul may be denied or buried in the unconscious personality layers of mother, father and child. That's the challenge, the risk, the testing—and the learning.

As soon as the first step into biological form is taken, at conception, the veils of forgetting, the sheaths of conditioning, come in and layer on during the entire prenatal epoch, culminating with great intensity at the trauma of birth, especially if this occurs with little or no consideration for the consciousness and spiritual nature of the child. The processes of conditioning and forgetting continue of course, during infancy, childhood and formative years, during which inherited predispositions are combined with conditioned reaction patterns.

Soul-memories tend to fade progressively with age. In William Wordsworth's poem *Intimations of Immortality from Recollections of Early Childhood*, he expresses beautifully the spiritual origin of the soul and the progressive, but not complete, forgetting of the formative years:

> *Our birth is but a sleep and a forgetting*
> *The Soul that rises with us, our life's Star*
> *Hath had elsewhere its setting,*
> *And cometh from afar:*
> *Not in entire forgetfulness,*

> *And not in utter nakedness,*
> *But trailing clouds of glory do we come*
> *From God, who is our home;*
> *Heaven lies about us in our infancy!*

And yet, at every moment of this whole process, this whole life, the possibility of remembering our true origin, and re-connecting to our soul and its purpose arises. As I related in Chapter Two, with conscious, spiritual conception and birthing attitudes and practices, the soul connection may be maintained, or re-established. William Emerson and his colleagues tell the following beautiful story:

> A four-year-old girl kept asking to be alone with her newborn sibling. At first the parents were worried that she might harm the baby out of sibling jealousy. They finally agreed to the girl's request, but listened via intercom from the next room. After a period of silence, they heard their daughter say to the baby, "Tell me about heaven. I'm beginning to forget." (Linn, Emerson, et al. *Remembering our Home*, p. 31).

In my divination ritual workshops I've observed that sometimes, tuning in to the memory of one's earliest experience of the bonding-gazing between newborn infant and mother, can lead directly to the recognition and remembrance of the communion of two souls. On the other hand, some people, when asked to recall the first bonding-gazing experience, will remember sensing anxiety, coldness or even hatred in the mother's eyes. Clearly, they are then recalling a painful moment in which the soul communion was temporarily obstructed. The residues of such pain would then first need to be healed.

The passage of the soul from incarnational choice to conception and then birth may be reflected in dreams and visionary communications between parents-to-be and the child soul around the time of conception and discovery. Such dream visitations heralding a soul's arrival are typically accompanied by deep feelings of peaceful joy, and a sense of expansive spiritual awareness. Certainly this was true for my wife and myself, when we realized that the soul incarnating as our child had just announced its arrival in the maternal womb.

This expansive spiritual awareness associated with conscious recognition of the arrival of a soul is the archetypal theme of the *Annunciation.* In Luke's gospel story of the birth of Jesus, after the Angel Gabriel has announced to Mary that she will give birth to a "Son of the Highest," she visits her cousin Elizabeth, who is pregnant with the future John the Baptist. Elizabeth says she feels her baby "leap in her womb." Mary says "My soul magnifies the Lord." *(Magnificat anima mea Dominum).* The *Magnificat* prayer has provided the text for some of the most sublime religious music in the Western liturgical tradition.

Some parents have extensive conversations/negotiations with their child's soul, and dream visions of that child's future. Sometimes other relatives, like the mother's mother, or an attendant midwife or friend, may have dream communications with the unborn child. Usually, in such dream encounters, the soul announcing its arrival is seen as a young child, or sometimes an adult, not an embryo, fetus or infant. Such visionary encounters with the souls of unborn children confirm that at the level of soul or essence the outer distinctions between adult and child are irrelevant. All souls are equal in the eyes and heart of the Divine.

As numerous stories collected and recorded in the books by Elizabeth Hallett and Sarah Hinze attest, a kind of dialogue of agreement occurs around the conception, and may be recalled in dreams of the parents. Sometimes there is a clear sense of the soul choosing the parents, and parents agreeing – at other times there is negotiating, communication and accommodating. The soul may announce its future appearance, gender and even name. Sometimes a mother may feel unready for a birth, but insistent, repeated dream visitations from a future child fills them with peaceful, loving expansiveness and wonder.

Even the occurrence of conception, discovery and annunciation however does not preclude further choices and changes. Parents may dream a child soul requesting to be accepted – and parents may accept the conception, or postpone it, or "close the womb door" to the soul applying to be born, in the language of the *Bardo Thödol*. After conception has occurred and an embryo begun to develop, miscarriages may still be chosen by the unborn child, and communicated in dreams to the parents, as we have seen. Miscarriage may be a soul's choice out of compassion for the mother or in recognition of an expected difficulty in the circumstances.

Some parents, especially with the newer initiatives with conscious, spiritual birthing practices, are able to maintain the conscious soul connection even through and after birth. More commonly, at some point in the pregnancy there is a separation of the transcendent soul-awareness and the more limited fetal awareness.

> A pregnant woman related having frequent empathic conversations with the adult-seeming being residing in her womb – conversations about her health concerns, diet, etc, like two adult friends planning a project together. After a certain point in the pregnancy, the woman suddenly began to feel alone and abandoned by her friend – until she got the message that the soul needed to concentrate on being more closely involved with the growing fetus, preparing for the potentially difficult passage of birth (Hallett, E., *Stories of the Unborn Soul*).

Tibetan Buddhist teachings on the bardo of rebirth

Although the *Bardo Thödol* does not explicitly mention the prenatal epoch as such, we can find in the teachings of the after-death *bardo* states some suggestive parallels with findings now emerging out of the work of prenatal and past-life regression therapists and highly developed intuitives. In this phase, also called the *bardo of seeking a new life,* the traveler in the intermediate realms is repeatedly admonished to remember where he is, and that his thoughts and intentions will profoundly affect the kind of experience he/she may have in his new life.

He is told that he is not in his ordinary body, but a "mental body," or "*bardo* body," or "desire body," which can't be killed, but which can fly, pass through walls, and has all kinds of non-ordinary capacities. In other words, he/she is in what are also called, in esoteric traditions, the intermediate planes (astral-emotional and mental-noetic), descending step by step to the time-space material level of existence.

The soul is then reminded of the six possible *lokas* (worlds) of *samsara* (existence) into which he might find him or herself drifting, carried along by the karmic propensities of their previous existence. Here the teachings of the *Bardo Thödol* converge with the teachings represented in the *Wheel of Samsara* with its six possible realms or states of consciousness in which we may find ourselves – after death, but also during life. Francesca Freemantle, a student of Trungpa Rinpoche, writes in her book on the *Tibetan Book of the Dead,*

> Many Western Buddhists have difficulties with the concept of rebirth in the six realms, or even with rebirth at all. No one can prove to us what lies beyond death. However, we *can* investigate our minds here and now and discover all the worlds contained within. We can find out what life as a hu-

man being really means at this very moment...Trungpa Rinpoche always spoke of the six realms as states of mind, and emphasized the importance of understanding them in this way while we have the opportunity in this life (Freemantle, F. *Luminous Emptiness*, p. 143-144).

I will discuss the six realms and the *Wheel of Births and Deaths* in more detail in a subsequent volume of this series, but mention here only briefly the chief characteristics and qualities of these realms – how *we* (human beings) come into these realms through our unconscious karmic tendencies.

The *hell realm* is marked by claustrophobic feelings of suffering and victimization, caused by aggression.

The *pretas realm* of "hungry ghosts" is a world of frustrated craving and unsatisfied desire, symbolized by the distended stomachs but thin mouths of the spirits in this realm.

The *animal realm* is a world of focusing on survival instincts – food, sex, sleep, self-preservation, with lack of aspiration for higher values.

The *realm of asuras,* often translated as "jealous gods" or "titans," is a world of struggle, competition and violence, into which we come through discontent, jealousy and grasping envy.

The *world of devas or gods* is a realm of cultivating pleasure and aesthetic delight of the senses, which in the Buddhist view is a temporary state of indulgent self-satisfaction.

The *human realm* is described by Trungpa as "the epitome of communication and relationship," in which there is curiosity for knowledge and aspiration for spiritual values. It has some of the qualities of all the other realms, but is less fixated and bound than those.

In the *Bardo Thödol* the *bardo* traveller is admonished to avoid being caught or driven into any of the realms, but if unavoidable to aim intention either for the *deva* realm or the human realm. The human world is considered the best of the six to be born into – because it offers the "precious opportunity" of liberation and enlightenment. The remaining instructions in the *bardo of rebirth* phase of the after-death journey deal with instructions on how to first delay being born at all, and then to choose the best kind of human birth.

The guidance for the soul embarking on its journey into a new incarnation are couched as instructions on how to "close the womb-door," – the point here being to delay the rebirth as long as possible, so that one can avoid being sucked into unfavorable births by one's unconscious karmic propensities *(samskaras)*. The first method of closing the womb-door is to remember that you are *in* this *bardo* of rebirth and focus on positive intentions: "holding in mind one single resolution, persist in joining up the chain of good karma…this is a time when earnestness and pure love are necessary."

The second, third, fourth and fifth methods of closing the womb-door all involve different ways of responding to visions of men and women copulating. The *bardo* traveler is urged not to join in, although he or she may be tempted to do so. It's as if the Buddhist masters are saying "Do not rush into a new incarnation. Staying with conscious intention at the very beginning is more likely to lead to a more conscious human lifetime."

I suggest that the *vision of a couple copulating is the vision of one's own conception.* This existential choice-point, where the soul chooses which couple to have as parents, can be reached in prenatal regression divinations, and is here arrived at from the other side, at the end of the after-life period, when the decision to re-incarnate has been made.

The *Bardo Thödol* says that if the voyager feels attraction to the female and aversion to the male, he will be reborn as a male; and if attraction to the male and aversion to the female, she will be born as female. As we now know from medical research, the gender of the child is determined in the earliest phases of embryonic development, and can involve all kinds of variations of genital anatomy. And as Sigmund Freud famously observed, "anatomy is destiny." Some scientists now believe the origin of the inclination to homosexuality may be in embryonic development. These scientific findings could be seen as consistent with a view that sees homosexuality, as well as gender and its variations, as soul choices made to provide certain learning conditions for that soul in its earthly-human existence.

If, even after using the various methods of preventing or postponing rebirth by meditating with conscious intention on light, and on one's chosen deity, one is still drawn into a womb for birth, the deceased is given instructions for "choosing of the womb-door." First there are "premonitory visions of the place of rebirth"– the continents in four directions are described, where one might be born. "All the places of birth will be known to you, one after another. Choose accordingly." The soul in the *bardo* of rebirth is advised to use their foresight to choose a human birth in an area in which religion and ethics prevail.

To *summarize,* the instructions of the *Bardo Thödol* for the most favorable kind of re-birth, are: to delay the return from the light- and wisdom-filled heaven worlds as long as possible, and when the time comes, which you know by seeing the acts of conception between men and women, to choose a birth family where the likelihood of coming into contact with the *dharma* teachings are greatest. The ending of the interlife period is the beginning of the *bardo* of rebirth: the decision is made to reincarnate, in a blending of karmic tendencies and conscious choice, and conception takes place in a fleshly human womb. This rebirth phase then ends with the actual physical birth, nine months later, when we start cycling through the three *bardos* of waking life, dreaming and meditating. In conclusion, below is my version of the Root-Verse for the *bardo* of rebirth:

> *Now, as the bardo of rebirth dawns upon me,*
> *I will hold one-pointedly to a single wish –*
> *Continuously directing intention with a positive outlook.*
> *Delaying the return to Earth-Life as long as possible.*
> *I will concentrate on pure energy and love,*
> *And cast off jealousy while meditating*
> *on the Guru Father-Mother.*

The Angel Lailah – Midwife of Souls

In Chapter Three we encountered Lailah as the guide to the after-life. In the vast literature of Jewish mystical teaching stories referred to as *midrashim*, there are references to the activities of an "angel of conception," also called "midwife of souls", which illuminate the points made here about the process of incarnation. Talmudic scholar and translator Daniel Matt pointed out to me (in a letter) that the name *Lailah* means "Night" in Hebrew, and that this angel is elsewhere in the Zohar identified with Gabriel. In the Gospel stories Gabriel is the messenger of the Annunciation, announcing the conception of John to Zachariah, and of the Christ child to Mary.

Some versions of the story of Lailah emphasize the reluctance or resistance of the soul to entering into human life, which seems to contradict the notion of incarnational choice. It is however consistent with the observation that, associated with the memory of our original abode, there is often a kind of divine homesickness or sense of alienation.

> Among the angels there is one who serves as midwife of souls. This is Lailah, the angel of conception. When the time has come for conception, Lailah seeks out a certain soul hidden in the Garden of Eden and commands it to enter the seed. The soul is always reluctant, for it still remembers the pain of being born, and it prefers to remain pure. But Lailah compels the soul to obey, and that is how new life comes into being.
>
> While the infant grows in the womb, Lailah watches over it, reading the unborn child the history of its soul. All the while a light shines upon the head of the child, by which it sees from one end of the world to the other. And Lailah shows the child the rewards of the Garden of Eden, and the punishments of Gehenna (Schwartz, H. *Before You Were Born*, p. 57).

So here is the image of the soul reluctantly leaving its heavenly abode, and being sent on a mission into the world. The soul is assisted by an angelic guide, who tells it the history of its previous incarnations, and provides it with divine foreknowledge, as well as a scenario of likely consequences of good and bad actions. The guidance from the Angel Lailah even precedes the actual conception (entering into the seed); and then continues during the prenatal period.

The *Zohar's* version of this extraordinary tale does not mention any reluctance on the part of the soul to enter into form, but does make it clear that the soul is originally androgynous, and only becomes polarized as male or female on the descent into human form.

> Rabbi Abba said: Happy are the righteous whose souls are hidden away with the Holy King before they come into the world! For so we have learned: At the moment the blessed Holy One brings forth souls into the world, all those spirits and souls comprise male and female joined as one. They are transmitted into the hands of the emissary appointed over human con-

ception. As they descend and are entrusted to him, they separate – sometimes one preceding the other – and he deposits them into human beings (Matt, D. *The Zohar: Pritzker Edition*, 2003).

Both variants of the story mention that the birth is painful, and this pain is the cause of soul's forgetting its origin. This is certainly consistent with the observations from the studies of the effects of birth trauma – that it causes massive amnesia.

A fascinating detail of the story involving the Angel Lailah occurs only in the version reported by Schwartz, which is said to have originated in the Babylonian period around the 9th century. After using the light above the head to show the unborn the rewards of the Garden of Eden and the punishments of Gehenna (as cited above) –

> When the time has come to be born, the angel Lailah extinguishes the light and brings forth the child into the world, and as it is brought forth, it cries. Then Lailah lightly strikes the newborn above the lip, causing it to forget all it has learned. And that is the origin of this mark, which everyone bears (Schwartz, H. op. cit. p. 58).

There is a puzzle with this story. According to folklore, touching with the finger on the philtrum above the upper lip is a gesture we make when trying to remember something. I encourage the reader to try it. It makes more sense that the compassionate gesture of the Angel Lailah, the angel that guides the soul into this world, is a gesture to help us remember our origin when we are *in extremis*, rather than a gesture of forgetting, or closing off the connection to the higher worlds. In other words, I suggest that the *philtrum is a point of remembrance, not forgetting.*

When I related this puzzling observation to my friend, acupuncturist Susan Fox, she pointed out that in traditional Chinese medicine, this point at the philtrum, above the upper lip just below the nose, called *Governor Vessel .26*, is considered a point of "consciousness," to be stimulated when reviving someone who is unconscious.

> The Governor Vessel (which comes up the back from the tailbone, over the top of the head, the nose, and then ends under the lip) governs all the *yang* channels, and the nose which receives heavenly chi, both correspond to heaven (yang). The Conception Vessel (which comes up from the pubic bone and terminates at the lower lip) is the central *yin* channel. Thus, this point is said to establish the connection between heaven (yang) and earth (yin), and is also called "man's middle," since man (the human) is situated between heaven and earth (Deadman, P. & Al-Khafaji, M. *Manual of Acupuncture*. p. 559).

With this unexpected confirmation from a completely different and independent system of subtle energy anatomy, I feel there is some support for interpreting the action of the Angel Lailah, the guiding angel of incarnation and conception, as setting us up with a gesture of conscious remembering, for reminding us of our true nature as souls. One could practice it that way.

Since I do not understand the Hebrew language and have only an outsider's acquaintance with the literature of Jewish mysticism, I was naturally a bit tentative about my interpretation of this story of the Angel Lailah. I asked my old friend and mentor Rabbi Zalman Schachter-Shalomi, who has long had an interest in consciousness studies, to comment on my reading of this tale. He offered the following (Schachter-Shalomi, personal communication, 2004):

> The puzzle of the psyche has engaged many people. Some of them have contended that we come in as a tabula rasa, while others have contended that we enter into our bodies with some imprint from before. Finding the tale of angel Lailah, Ralph Metzner has immersed himself in the worlds of midrashic and Kabbalistic literature. His reading of this myth differs from the usual literary analysis, he is aware of the realities behind the words of the tale. It is important to understand that we always bring our ethnic and cultural imagery to our understanding of these myths. By reaching into the accounts of shamans and mystics we seek to encounter the reality behind their words. And each epistemology we will bring different descriptions.

Academic epistemologies tend to look at things as objects or ideas. As we enter the realm Dr. Metzner brings to this study, we begin to move from a merely conceptual epistemology to a participatory one. This requires that we imaginally regress to our own origins. In this way we are a step closer to the realization of our existence. Enjoy the journey!

* * *

This incarnational journey of the human soul, from heaven or the spirit world, into biological form at conception, then birth, growth and development, with the attendant high probabilities of total soul-forgetting in the attachments and cravings of the material sense world --- all this is expressed in a poetic allegory called *The Hymn of the Pearl,* which is part of a Gnostic text known as *The Acts of Thomas,* dating from the fourth century.

The original name of the Gnostic poem – *The Hymn of the Soul* – makes clear that we are dealing with the story of the incarnational journey. We are told of a royal couple, called the "Father of Truth" and the "Mother of Wisdom," who send their son out from the "House of the Highest Ones," on a long and perilous journey, to find and retrieve the One Pearl, guarded by a fierce serpent. "They made a covenant with me, and wrote it in my heart, so I would not forget."

The son is symbolic of the human soul, going out from the heaven realm of the Divine Father-Mother, into a human life journey, with a contract and a mission. The son-soul has to give up his royal raiments, symbolic of the higher, etheric "light-bodies," and take on the clothing of the people in "Egypt," symbolic of the material sense world. He gets involved with people, forgets about the dragon and the pearl, forgets he is the son of royal parents, and eats the food and drink the people give him.

"Through the heaviness of their food, I fell into a deep sleep." In other words, he becomes attached, addicted and unconscious of his true spiritual nature. Then there is a turning point.

He receives a message from his parents – a magical letter, that "rose up in the form of an eagle…that flew and alighted beside me, and became speech. At its voice and the sound of its rustling, I awoke and rose from my sleep." The letter tells him – "Awake and rise from your sleep. Remember that you are a son of Kings and see the slavery of your life." He remembers his mission – finding and pacifying the serpent and retrieving the pearl. He proceeds on his homeward journey, the classic return journey of the mystic seeker. The letter that had "awakened me with its voice, now guided me with its light."

He finds again the "robe of glory, glowing with sapphires and many colors," that he had left behind when he left his heavenly home. The multi-colored robe is undoubtedly a symbolic reference to the light-fire energy-field, that provides him with insight and self-knowledge. "I saw it quiver all over with the movements of *gnosis*… As I gazed on it, the garment itself seemed to be a mirror of myself. I saw in it my whole self, and I saw myself apart – we were two entities, yet one form."

A prayer-poem by Rainer Maria Rilke also beautifully expresses the moment of incarnational choice and the sense of guidance from the divine spirit that is given at that choice point – and available for us to remember at any point in life – if we are receptive. The translation below is from *Rilke's Book of Hours*, by Anita Barrows and Joanna Macy.

God speaks to each of us as he makes us,
then walks silently out of the night.

These are the words we dimly hear:

You sent out beyond your recall,
go to the limits of your longing.
Embody me.

Flare up like flame
and make big shadows I can move in.

Let everything happen to you: beauty and terror.
Just keep going. No feeling is final.
Don't let yourself lose me.

Nearby is the country they call life.
You will know it by its seriousness.

Give me your hand.

References and Select Bibliography

Introduction

Grof, Stanislav. and Grof, Christina. *Holotropic Breathwork – A New Approach to Self-Exploration and Therapy*. Albany, NY: SUNY Press. 2010. With numerous color illustrations. Exposition of the breathwork method of consciousness exploration, by the founding pioneers of this method.

Leskowitz, Eric (editor) *Transpersonal Hypnosis – Gateway to Body, Mind and Spirit*. Boca Raton, FL: CRC Press, 2000. A collection of essays describing hypnotic methods for accessing the spiritual/transpersonal dimensions of consciousness.

Lucas, Winafred (editor) *Regression Therapy: Handbook for Professionals*. 2 vols. Crest Park, CA: Deep Forest Press, 1993. Compendium of essays on hypnotic regression therapy and its various applications, including infancy, prenatal and past life therapy, by a wise and very experienced psychologist.

Metzner, Ralph. *Mind Space and Time Stream – Navigating Your States of Consciousness for Healing and Guidance*. Berkeley, CA: Regent Press , 2009.

Birth and the Prenatal Period – Chapters One and Two

APPPAH (Association for Pre- and Perinatal Psychology and Health). The APPPAH publishes a quarterly journal; as well as a catalogue of 100 books and video-tapes on the psychology of prenates and newborns, pregnancy, childbirth and infancy. [www.birthpsychology.com]

Castellino, Raymond. *The Polarity Therapy Paradigm Regarding Pre-Conception, Prenatal and Birth Imprinting*. 1995, 60 pp. Exposition of Castellino's brilliant and sensitive work with neonates and prenatal existence. [www.castellinotraining.com]

Chamberlain, David. *The Mind of Your Newborn Baby*. Berkeley: North Atlantic Books, 1988/1998. Lucid overview of the research with hypnotherapy that demonstrates that newborns and unborn fetuses are conscious human beings, who can perceive, feel, understand and communicate about their environment and the world in sophisticated ways.

Chamberlain, David. "Communicating with the Mind of a Prenate: Guidelines for Parents and Birth Professionals." *Journal of Prenatal and Perinatal Psychology and Health*, 18(2), p. 95-108, 2003.

Dass, Ram and Metzner, Ralph with Bravo, Gary. *Birth of a Psychedelic Culture.* Santa Fe, NM: Synergetic Press, 2010. A conversational memoir of the Harvard studies with psychedelics and the community experiments in Millbrook, NY, in the early 1960s.

DeMause, Lloyd. *The Foundations of Psychohistory*. New York: Creative Roots, Inc.: 1982. The founder of the psychohistory movement explains his methodology and the primary findings on the origins of violence in birth trauma and child abuse.

DeMause, Lloyd. (editor) *Journal of Psychohistory* [www.psychohistory.com]

Emerson, William. *Emerson Training Seminars*. Information on the teaching work of this pioneer pre- and peri-natal therapist, who works with regressing adults; but also with neonates and infants to heal the effects of traumatic birth. [www.emersonbirthrx.com]

English, Jane. *Different Doorway – Adventures of a Caesarean Born*. Pt. Reyes, CA: Earth Heart, 1985. Fascinating account of the inner world of the Caesarean born child – and how their uniquely different birth experience shapes adult life.

Grof, Stanislav. *Realms of the Human Unconscious*. New York: E.P. Dutton, 1976. An early statement of Grof's ground-breaking therapeutic and theoretical work.

Grof, Stanislav. *The Psychology of the Future: Lessons from Modern Consciousness Research*. Albany, NY: State University of New York (SUNY) Press., 2000.

Hallett, Elizabeth. *Stories of the Unborn Soul: The Mystery and Delight of Pre-Birth Communication*. San José, CA: Writer's Club Press, 2002. An extraordinary collection of pre-birth experience stories told by astonished parents who spontaneously experienced communications with the unborn souls of their children, in dreams and waking state visions.

Hellinger, Bert. *Love's Hidden Symmetry – What Makes Love Work in Relationships*. Phoenix, AZ: Zeig, Tucker & Co., 1998. The first comprehensive English-language presentation of Hellinger's innovative and far-reaching work with family constellations.

Hellinger, Bert. *On Life and Other Paradoxes – Aphorisms and Little Stories*. translated and with an Introduction by Ralph Metzner. Phoenix, AZ: Zeig, Tucker & Co., 2002. Little gems of insight from the master of family systems healing work. Also contains examples of the "statements of empowerment" he suggests people use in healing dysfunctional relationships in families through representatives.

Hinze, Sarah. *Coming from the Light.* New York: Pocket Books, 1994. Janus, Ludwig. *The Enduring Effects of Prenatal Experience: Echoes from the Womb.* Northvale, NJ: Aronson. 1997. More amazing true stories of dreams and waking state communications between souls before and around birth.

Johnson, Jessica & Odent, Michel. *We Are All Water Babies.* Berkeley, CA: Celestial Arts, 1995. A book of spectacularly beautiful photographs of birth in water, ecstatic babies swimming joyfully under water with their parents and with dolphins.

Leboyer, Frederic. *Birth Without Violence.* New York: Knopf, 1975. The pioneering French obstetrician's first published statement of his revolutionary approach to non-traumatic, natural child-birthing.

Linn, Sheila Fabricant, William Emerson, Dennis Linn, Matthew Linn. *Remembering Our Home – Healing Hurts & Receiving Gifts From Conception to Birth.* Mahwah, NJ: Paulist Press, 1999. An exposition of Emerson's pre-birth and birth trauma work, linked symbolically with the archetypal story of the conception and birth of Jesus.

McGoldrick, Monica, Randy Gerson, Sylvia Shellenberger. *Genograms – Assessment and Intervention.* New York: W.W. Norton & Co., 1999. Textbook on the methods of using genograms in family systems therapy.

Metzner, Ralph (editor) *Wetland Apes: The Missing Link? A Fresh Look at Aquatic Ape Theory.* Special issue of *ReVision – Journey of Consciousness and Transformation.* Vol 15, No. 2, Fall 1995. With essays by Elaine Morgan, Michel Odent, Derek Ellis, Derek Denton, Michael Crawford, Marc Verhaegen and Roger Wescott.

Metzner, Ralph. *The Roots of War and Domination.* Berkeley, CA: Regent Press, 2008. In this book I discuss what I have called the "curse of Yahweh" in more detail, relating it to the writings of Zachariah Sitchin, the Sumerologist, who argues that Biblical and other ancient creation myths reflect the history of our interaction with long-lived ET "gods" (called Annunaki in Sumerian and Nefilim in Hebrew) from the planet Nibiru, who colonized Earth and hybridized our hominid ancestors. The two leaders of the Annunaki were at first Enki, a benevolent creator craftsman associated with water, and in a later period his brother Enlil, a stern law-giver who operated a slave colony in Eden, until he evicted the hybridized humans for disobedience, forcing them to live in a desert environment for which they were poorly adapted.

Morgan, Elaine. *The Scars of Evolution.* London: Souvenir Press, 1994. Elaine Morgan is an independent scholar and researcher and one of the main proponents of what is known as the aquatic ape theory of human evolution.

Murray, Henry A. *Endeavors in Psychology – Selections from the Personology of Henry A. Murray.* New York: HarperCollins, 1981.

Odent, Michel. *Birth Reborn.* New York: Pantheon Books, 1984.

Orr, Leonard & Ray, Sondra. *Rebirthing in the New Age.* Berkeley, CA: Celestial Arts, 1983.

Rank, Otto. *The Trauma of Birth.* New York: Harcourt Brace, 1929.

Rank, Otto. *The Myth of the Birth of the Hero.* 1909. Johns Hopkins Univ. Press., 2004.

Reich, Wilhelm. *Character Analysis.* New York: Farrar, Strauss & Giroux, 1949. Classic exposition, by one of Freud's most brilliant students, of the process of character formation through muscular armoring. "The muscular armor is functionally equivalent to the character defenses," was his summary statement.

Verny, Thomas, with John Kelly. *The Secret Life of the Unborn Child.* New York: Dell Publishing, 1981/1986. Summary overview of two decades of research on the conscious life and experience of unborn children.

Films

Vladimirova, Elena. *Birth as We Know It.* The work of the Russian waterbirth collective was first presented in a 30 min film called *Birth Into Being.* This is an 80 min film on the same group, including the spiritual midwife Tatyana Sargunas and nine other women, birthing in water tanks and at the Black Sea, with dolphins. With 2 hours of extra features, it is one of the most inspiring films I have ever seen, offering a vision of a life in harmony with Nature and Spirit. [www.birthintobeing.com]

Takikawa, Debby. *What Babies Want.* Featuring interviews with Joseph Chilton Pearce, David Chamberlain, Barbara Findeisen, Ray Castellino and others. This film is an exploration of the consciousness of infants. [www.whatbabieswant.com]

Death and the After-Life – Chapters Three and Four

Botkin, Allan. *Induced After Death Communication.* Charlottesville, VA: Hampton Roads, 2005. A VA psychologist working with traumatized soldiers unexpectedly discovered communication with deceased souls while using the eye-movement desensitization technique (EMDR).

Evans-Wentz, W.Y. (ed). *The Tibetan Book of the Dead.* Oxford University Press, 1960 (first publisched 1927). The classic translation, used by Leary, Alpert and myself in our psychedelic adaptation.

Fechner, Gustav Theodor. "The Little Book of Life After Death", in *Journal of Pastoral Counseling*, Annual, Vol. XXVII, 1992. Translation of: *Das Büchlein vom Leben nach dem Tode*, first published in 1836 in Germany, under the pseudonym "Mises." The *Insel-Bücherei* published it as No. 187 of their series, with a *Geleitwort* by Wilhelm Wundt, one of the founding fathers of experimental psychology. A new edition of the *Büchlein*, together with *Vergleichende Anatomie der Engel*, was published in 1980 by Age d'Homme – Karolinger, Wien.

Fremantle, Francesca. *Luminous Emptiness – Understanding the Tibetan Book of the Dead*. Boston & London: Shmabhala, 2003. A lucid analysis of the mythology and iconography of the *Bardo Thödol*, by a disciple of the late Chögyam Trungpa.

Grant, Joan. *Winged Pharaoh* (originally published 1937). Columbus, OH: Ariel Press edition, 1985. This is one of six historical novels, which JG regarded as autobiographies of her past lives, recalled through "far memory." Together with her husband Denys Kelsey, a psychiatrist doing past-life regression therapy, she also wrote *Many Lifetimes*, a fascinating account of their work together.

Grob, C.S. The use of psilocybin in patients with advanced cancer and existential anxiety: in Winkelman, M., and Roberts, T. (Eds.) *Psychedelic Medicine: New Evidence for Hallucinogens as Treatments*. Westport, CT, Praeger/Greenwood, vol. 1, p. 205-216, 2007.

Grob, C.S, Danforth, A.L, Chopra, G.S, Hagerty, M.C, McKay, C.R, Halberstadt, A.L. and Greer, G.R. A pilot study of psilocybin treatment for anxiety in patients with advanced-stage cancer. *Archives of General Psychiatry, Online*, September 6, 2010.

Grof, Stanislav & Halifax, Joan. *The Human Encounter with Death*. New York: E.P. Dutton, 1977.

Heagerty, N. Riley (ed.) *The French Revelation – The Extaordinary Eyewitness Account of the Pschic Wonder of Rochester – Emily French*. Kearney, NE: Morris Publishing, 1995.

Huxley, Aldous. *Island*. London/NewYork: Harper, 1962.

Huxley, Laura. *This Timeless Moment – A Personal View of Aldous Huxley*. Corte Madera, CA: Celestial Arts, 1968.

Kelsey, Denys & Grant, Joan. *Many Lifetimes*. Garden City, NJ: Doubleday, 1967.

Lamy, Lucie. *Egyptian Mysteries*. New York: Crossroad. 1981. A richly illustrated guide to Egyptian after-death teachings, by a disciple of famed Egyptologist, R. A. Schwaller de Lubicz.

Leary. Timothy, Ralph Metzner & Richard Alpert. *The Psychedelic Experience – A Manual Based on the Tibetan Book of the Dead.* New Hyde Park, N,Y,: University Books, 1964.

Leland, Kurt. *The Unanswered Question – Death, Near-Death and the Afterlife.* Charlottesville, VA: Hampton Roads, 2002.

Levine, Stephen. *Who Dies? An Investigation of Conscious Living and Conscious Dying.* Garden City, NJ: Doubleday Anchor Books, 1982. Stephen Levine's books on assisting and preparing for dying are beautifully sensitive and compassionate meditations. I have reread this one several times.

Metzner, Ralph. *The Well of Remembrance – Remembering the Earth-Wisdom Myths of Northern Europe.* Boston & London: Shambhala, 1994.

Metzner, Ralph. *Green Psychology.* Rochester, VT: Park Street Press, 1999. See especially Chapter 9: "The Black Goddess, the Green God and the Wild Human" for discussions of Isis and Osiris

Metzner, Ralph. *The Unfolding Self – Varieties of Transformative Experience.* Novato, CA; Origin Press, 1998. See especially Chapter 7 – "On Dying and Being Reborn."

Metzner, Ralph. "Homage to the Visionary Toad." In: Krassner, Paul (ed.) *Magic Mushrooms and Other Highs.* 2003 [www.paulkrassner.com]

Moody, Raymond. *ReUnions – Visionary Encounters with Departed Loved Ones.* New York: Willard Books, 1993.

Newton, Michael. *Journey of Souls – Case Studies of Life Between Lives.* St. Paul, MN: Llewellyn Publications, 1994.

Newton, Michael. *Destiny of Souls – New Case Studies of Life Between Lives.* St. Paul, MN: Llewellyn Publications, 2000.

Ring, Kenneth. *The Omega Project – Near-Death Experiences, UFO Encounters, and Mind At Large.* New York: Quill William Morrow, 1992.

Ring, Kenneth. *Lessons from the Light.* Portsmouth, NH: Moment Point Press, 1998. This is Ken Ring's last and most profound collection of NDE experiences.

Thurman, Robert. *The Tibetan Book of the Dead.* New York: Bantam Books, 1994. A newer translation of this ancient text. Although I am not a Tibetan language scholar, I find the Evans-Wentz translation more meaningful. According to Robert Thurman, the title of the work should more accurately read *The Great Book of Natural Liberation Through Understanding in the Between.* "Between" (as a noun) is Thurman's translation of the term *bardo* – a somewhat odd linguistic choice for the concept which Evans-Wentz translated as "intermediate state."

Wasson, R. Gordon, Hofmann, Albert & Ruck, Carl A.P. *The Road to Eleusis – Unveiling the Secret of the Mysteries.* Berkeley, CA: North Atlantic Books. 1978/2008.

Websites

The Vaults of Erowid – An outstanding information resource for all aspects of psychedelic and psychoactive plants and drugs. *[www. erowid.org[*

Chapter Five – From Incarnation to Conception and Rebirth

Arrien, Angeles. *The Four-Fold Way – Walking the Paths of the Warrior, Teacher, Healer and Visionary.* HarperSanFrancisco, 1993.

Barrows, Anita & Macy, Joanna (transl.) *Rilke's Book of Hours – Love Poems to God.* NY: Riverhead Books (G.P.Putnam's), 1996.

Browne, Sylvia. *Life on the Other Side – A Psychic's Tour of the After-Life.* NY: New American Library, 2000.

Deadman, Peter & Al-Khafaji, Mazin. *A Manual of Acupuncture.* Hove, East Sussex, UK: Journal of Chinese Medicine Publications, 1998. According to the authors of this treatise, stimulating this point "restores consciousness and calms the spirit." Among it's indications are "sudden loss of consciousness, coma, acute and chronic childhood fright…mania-depression, epilepsy, (and) wasting and thirsting disorder." The authors say "when the harmonious interaction of *yin* and *yang* is lost and they begin to separate, there is loss of consciousness (death being the ultimate manifestation of this separation)…Renzhong DU-26 was indicated for resuscitation, and it is the single most important acupuncture point to revive consciousness and re-establish yin-yang harmony." (p. 559-560).

Hymn of the Pearl. Also called *Hymn of the Soul.* From the Gnostic *Acts of Thomas.* In: Barnstone, Willis (ed). *The Other Bible – Ancient Esoteric Texts from the Pseudepigrapha, the Dead Sea Scrools, the early Kabbalah, the Nag Hammadi Library and other sources.* San Francisco: Harper & Row,1984. (p.308-313).

Macy, Joanna & Brown, Molly. *Coming Back to Life – Practices to Reconnect Our Lives, Our World.* Gabriola Island, BC: New Society Publishers, 1998. "The *Bodhisattva Check-In* is inspired by the Buddhist teaching of the bodhisattva. Embodying our motivation to serve, the bodhisattva does not seek enlightenment to exit from this world of woe, but turns back…having vowed to return again and again to be of help to all beings…The bodhisattva archetype is present in all religions and even all social movements, be it in the guise of suffering servant, worker-priest, shaman, prophet, idealistic revolutionary, or community organizer." (p. 130).

Matt, Daniel C. (transl. & commentary) *The Zohar: Pritzker Edition*. Palo Alto, CA: Stanford University Press, 2003. (2 volumes).

Myss, Caroline. *Sacred Contracts: Awakening Your Divine Potential*. Three Rivers Press, 2003.

Schwartz, Howard. *Gabriel's Palace – Jewish Mystical Tales*. NY: Oxford University Press, 1993.

Schwartz, Howard. *Before You Were Born*. (illustr. Kristina Swarner). Brookfield, CT.: Roaring Brook Press, 2005.

Appendix

On the mediumship of William Shakespeare

Let me give the most remarkable illustration of spirit suggestion – the immortal Shakespeare. Neither of his parents could read or write. He grew up in a small village among ignorant people, on the banks of the Avon. There was nothing in the peaceful, quiet landscape on which he looked, nothing in the low hills, the undulating fields, nothing in the lazy flowing stream to excite the imagination. Nothing in his early years calculated to sow the seeds of subtlest and sublimest thought. There was nothing in his education or lack of education to account for what he did. It is supposed that he attended school in his home village, but of that there is no proof. He went to London when young, and within a few years became interested in Black Friars Theater, where he was actor, dramatist, and manager. He was never engaged in a business counted reputable in that day. Socially, he occupied a position below servants. The law described him as a "sturdy vagabond." He died at 52.

How such a man could producd the works which he did has been the wonder of all time. Not satisfied that one with such limited advantages could possibly have written the masterpieces of literature, it has been by some contended that (Francis) Bacon was the author of all Shakespeare's comedies and tragedies.

It is a fact to be noted that in none of this man's plays is there any mention of his contemporaries. He made reference to no king, queen, poet, author, sailor, soldier, statesman or priest of his own period. He lived in an age of great deeds, in the time of religious wars, in the days of the armada, the edict of Nantes, the massare of St. Bartholomew, the victory of Leponto, the assasination of Henry III of France and the execution of Mary Stuart; yet he did not mention a single incident of his day and time.

The brain that conceived *Timon of Athens* was a Greek in the days of Pericles and familiar with the tragedies of that century. The mind that dictated *Julius Caesar* was an inhabitant of the Eternal City when Caesar led his legions in the field. The author of *Lear* was a pagan; of *Romeo and Juliet* an Italian who knew the ecstasies of love. The author of those plays must have been a physician, for he shows a knowledge of medicine and the symptoms of disease; a musician, for in

The Two Gentlemen of Verona he uses every musical term known to his contemporaries. He was a lawyer, for he was acquainted with the forms and expressions used by that profession. He was a botanist because he named nearly all known plants. He was an astronomer and a naturalist and wrote intelligently upon the stars and natural science. He was a sailor, or he could not have written *The Tempest*. He was a savage and trod the forest's silent depths. He knew all crimes, all regrets, all virtues, and their rewards. He knew the unspoken thoughts, desires and ways of beasts. He lived all lives. His brain was a sea on which the waves touch all the shores of experience. He was the wonder of his time and ours.

Was it possible for any man of his education and experience to conceive the things he did? All the Shakespearean works were, beyond a doubt, the product of his pen, but the conceptions, the plays, the tragedies were the work of many minds, given Shakespeare by spirit suggestion. He was the sensitive instrument through which a group of learned and distinguished scholars, inhabitants of many lands when in earth-life, gave to posterity the sublime masterpieces of the Bard of Avon.

(N. Riley Heagerty *The French Revelation*, p. 260-261)

Green Earth Foundation
Harmonizing Humanity with Earth and Spirit

The Green Earth Foundation is an educational and research organization dedicated to the healing and harmonizing of the relationships between humanity and the Earth, through a recognition of the energetic and spiritual interconnectedness of all life-forms in all worlds. Our strategic objectives are to help bring about changes in attitudes, values, perceptions, and worldviews that are based on ecological balance and respect for the integrity of all life. Our areas of research interest include consciousness studies, shamanism and Earth mythology, and green and eco-psychology. Green Earth Foundation also sponsors the *Metzner Alchemical Divination*® training program.

Green Earth Foundation
is producing and co-publishing a new series of books
by Ralph Metzner, Ph.D. –

THE ECOLOGY OF CONSCIOUSNESS

1. The Expansion of Consciousness
2. The Roots of War and Domination
3. Alchemical Divination
4. Mind Space and Time Stream
5. The Life Cycle of the Human Soul
6. Worlds Within and Worlds Beyond
7. The Six Life-Paths of the Human Soul

The Green Earth Foundation is a 501(c)(3) non-profit, educational and research organization. P.O. Box 327, El Verano, CA 95433. Internet: www.greenearthfound.org

Alchemical Divination

The *Metzner Alchemical Divination*® training program consists of three, modular 5-day workshops, in which one learns the divinations for oneself, and how to conduct them for others.

Janus and the Gateway of the Heart
- Mapping your Self-System and Life-World of Relations
- Finding your Orientation and Inner Direction
- Releasing Fear Blocks on Receiving and Expressing
- Connecting and Reconciling with your Ancestors and Elders
- The Six Archetypal Life-Paths of the Human Soul

Hermes and the Vessel of Transformation
- Mapping your Self-System and Life-World of Relations
- Relationship Disentanglement Divination
- Envisioning Possible/Probable Futures
- Reconciling with the Inner Enemy or Shadow
- Medicine Wheel of the Life Cycle

Mimir and the Well of Memory
- Mapping your Self-System and Life-World of Relations
- Finding and Connecting with your Spirit Guide
- Memory Divination for the Formative Years
- The Imprints of Conception and the Visions of the Soul
- The Tree of Self-Unfoldment

Each of the three workshops also includes a number of yogic-alchemical light-fire practices, designed to clear the perception channels, for the divinations. Participants who successfully complete all three workshops obtain a Certificate of Completion.

Please consult the website: www.metzneralchemicaldivination.org for details.

Metzner Alchemical Divination® is a registered trademark.

CPSIA information can be obtained at www.ICGtesting.com
Printed in the USA
LVOW042011081111

254072LV00001B/304/P